BIOGRAPHICAL SERIES · VOLUME I

THE NORWEGIAN-AMERICAN HISTORICAL
ASSOCIATION

Georg Sverdrup (1848-1907)
(Courtesy Augsburg College Archives)

Georg Sverdrup

Educator, Theologian, Churchman

by *James S. Hamre*

1986
The Norwegian-American Historical Association
NORTHFIELD • MINNESOTA

To Corrine

Foreword

This brief volume on the educator, theologian, and churchman Georg Sverdrup by James S. Hamre introduces a new series on Norwegian-American biography. It complements the association's *Authors Series*, which so far has six volumes, and it broadens the invitation for scholarly contributions about Norwegian Americans from many other walks of life.

It is our hope that the *Biographical Series* will eventually include a long list of carefully researched and sensitively interpreted studies of individuals whose lives and careers elucidate and expand our knowledge of a Norwegian presence and the dynamics of immigrant adjustment in America. In an eloquently formulated statement from 1960 the association's long-time editor, Kenneth O. Bjork, called for a renewed commitment to tell "the whole story of a transplanted people that is now deeply rooted in America," by a broad approach in our editorial selection policy. We are consequently obligated to give scholarly attention to the life situations of men and women in many occupational roles and callings, from pioneer toilers on the American frontier to captains of industry in the nation's great cities. And we need to know about persons in business, in the professions, in the arts, as religious and civic leaders, as inventors and founders of institutions, in charitable activity, and in numerous other endeavors.

Their stories may be told in collective or individual biographies; the field awaits the resourceful and interested researcher.

We are pleased to publish as volume one in the series this well-researched and thoughtfully written study of a prominent Norwegian American, whose qualities of leadership and influence reached far beyond his own immediate constituency to have an impact on attitudes and practices within American Lutheranism and religious life in general. It was, after all, the American environment that Georg Sverdrup found particularly appropriate and receptive to his theology, his ideas about church organization, and his principles of education. Sverdrup, who came to the United States in 1874, represented the new spiritual orientation in Norway and its transfer to America, associated with both a religious awakening and a greater democratic spirit. He held a firm conviction of a living Christianity within a free-church framework, with strongly independent congregations. His position as a professor and president at Augsburg Seminary, and the later college—from 1897 the schools of the newly formed Norwegian Lutheran Free Church—placed Sverdrup in a minority within an ethnic minority. His mission and achievements must be seen in such a context.

James S. Hamre is a professor in the department of religion at Waldorf College, Forest City, Iowa. He has lectured and published widely on topics relating to Norwegian-American religious and educational concerns, and he is a recognized authority on this subject.

In preparing the manuscript for publication, I enjoyed the competent and cordial assistance of Deborah L. Miller, who performed much of the demanding and detailed work of editing. To her go my heartfelt thanks. Gerald Lange of the Bieler Press in Minneapolis designed the volume; the index was prepared by Virginia L. Martin; and the edited manuscript was retyped by Juta M. Millert and Lois Nesseth. Their contributions are much appreciated.

Odd S. Lovoll
St. Olaf College

Preface

In the preface of his two-volume *Norwegian Migration to America*, Theodore C. Blegen stated that "the immigrant has been the focal point for the interplay of two creative forces in our national life, the European heritage and the American environment." This study explores one facet of that interplay: the religious forces that found expression in the person of Georg Sverdrup, an immigrant who came from Norway as a young man and played a leading role among his fellow immigrants.

I became seriously interested in Sverdrup in the fall of 1964. It was then that I enrolled as a graduate student in the School of Religion at the University of Iowa and, with the encouragement and direction of Professors Sidney E. Mead and Robert Michaelsen, I began work in the field of religion in American history. In 1967 I completed a doctoral dissertation that was primarily an annotated translation of certain of Sverdrup's key writings. That effort enabled me, as one who has been influenced by that tradition, to gain an understanding of the religious forces shaping Norwegian immigrants in America. My goal, however, has been to view these developments not just as isolated phenomena but as facets of the larger framework of the Protestant experience in America. I am especially indebted to Professors

Mead and Michaelsen for keeping before me this broader perspective.

Kenneth O. Bjork, former editor of the Norwegian-American Historical Association, was the first person to encourage me to undertake a biographical study of Sverdrup. More recently, Odd S. Lovoll, the present NAHA editor, has provided incentive and direction for the project. I want to take this opportunity to thank them for their many efforts.

I would also like to express my gratitude to the American Philosophical Society for a grant that made it possible for me to spend part of 1971 in Norway researching the Sverdrup family and nineteenth-century Norwegian intellectual and religious life. A fellowship from the National Endowment for the Humanities in 1974 enabled me to attend a summer seminar at the University of Illinois where I gained further understanding of the nineteenth-century debates in American higher education.

Anyone who does research in the field of religious developments among Norwegian immigrants recognizes at once that he builds on the work of others. The student of Sverdrup is especially indebted to the late Andreas Helland, who collected, edited, and published the six volumes of Sverdrup's writings under the title *Professor Georg Sverdrups samlede skrifter i udvalg*. His historical writings are also very useful, as are the essays and articles on Sverdrup by John O. Evjen. More recent works of great help are the studies by E. Clifford Nelson, Eugene L. Fevold, and Carl H. Chrislock. I am indebted to Professor Chrislock for helping me become familiar with the Augsburg College Archives and for reading substantial portions of an earlier manuscript of this study. Professor Fevold also kindly read the manuscript in its entirety and offered helpful comments. This work has benefited from their suggestions and insights. It goes without saying that any defects and mistakes found here cannot be charged to those scholars. I alone bear responsibility for them.

I would also like to thank the librarians and staff members of

Universitetsbiblioteket (Oslo), Augsburg College Library (Minneapolis), and Luther-Northwestern Theological Seminary Library (St. Paul) for their gracious assistance and consideration. I am also appreciative of the efforts of the Lutheran Historical Conference's Commission on Research and Publication whose members read the work and gave it their approbation.

Portions of chapters three, four, and six appeared in articles that were published earlier in *The Lutheran Quarterly, Norwegian-American Studies, Concordia Historical Institute Quarterly,* and *Luther Theological Seminary Review.*

Finally, a special word of thanks is due my wife, Corrine. Her patience and encouragement were essential to the completion of this project.

James S. Hamre
Waldorf College

Table of Contents

Georg Sverdrup

Educator, Theologian, Churchman

Introduction

"We stand here fully convinced that we are in more ways than one in the land of the future. We are certain that the Norwegian people have here a great and glorious task. It is to declare the truth that freedom is not apart from God but only in God, to bear witness that freedom and Christianity are not two things but one."[1]

Those words were spoken by Georg Sverdrup at a welcoming reception on August 25, 1874, just eight days after he and a colleague had arrived in Minneapolis from Norway to take up their duties as theological professors at Augsburg Seminary. In a sense these words presented him to his new home. A young man of twenty-five, Sverdrup was then briefly expressing what he believed to be the calling of the Norwegian people in America—and his own role in seeking to realize that calling. He devoted the remaining thirty-three years of his life to it.

In the annals of Norwegian Lutherans in America the name of Georg Sverdrup looms large. He was born into a distinguished family that had contributed a number of prominent leaders to Norwegian church and political life. Arriving in America in 1874, he threw himself into the task of building a "free congregation in a free church," by which he meant a local fellowship of believers within a church body in which such inhibiting factors as church hierarchy, clerical dominance, and secular law would no longer be problems. In such a setting both local congregation and church body would be free to realize their full potential. When Sverdrup died on May 3, 1907, it was clear to all—even those who had disagreed with him—that a man of stature and ability had passed from the scene.[2]

The words "educator," "theologian," and "churchman" may properly be applied to Georg Sverdrup. As an educator he consciously sought to create at Augsburg Seminary a school to serve the needs of the emancipated and vital congregations that he felt could be built in America. Such a school was to break with the European pattern in which the humanistic education received by the clergy had made them an aristocratic class that was not a part of the common people. The American setting, Sverdrup was convinced, offered the opportunity to create new forms. He held that to be truly useful, a seminary must foster and sustain the free church made possible in a democratic environment. That was the type of school he labored to build.

Sverdrup's theological stance was also closely linked to this central concern. By the time he arrived in America the Norwegian Lutherans in this country had organized into several groups, embodying some of the different accents and emphases that had been present in the Church of Norway. Sverdrup at once threw himself into the discussions and debates that were taking place. The foundation of his thinking was a belief in the above-mentioned free congregation in a free church, a view that he claimed was set forth in the New Testament and held by Martin Luther. He asserted that the papacy and the state churches had buried this concept. America, he was convinced, offered a setting in which the free church could be restored and rebuilt. He resisted with vigor those forces that he felt would stifle or interfere with the building of this kind of congregation. Sverdrup rejected what he regarded as an undue stress on "pure doctrine," with its emphasis on the theological system of Christianity, instead stressing an idea of the congregation as a living organism in which all of the gifts of the Holy Spirit would be used for the upbuilding and edification of the whole. The focus was to be on a new life in Christ rather than on form.

Sverdrup was not an ivory-tower theologian, however. His concerns and efforts were eminently practical. He was involved in the affairs of his church body and held definite views regarding church union. He served as an editor and contributed to newspapers, magazines, and journals read by Norwegian immigrants. He worked to promote interest in missions and was highly regarded both as a preacher and as a speaker. All of these activities reflected his intense conviction that builders of a free church needed to grasp the opportunity America offered.

By no means did Sverdrup's views and actions elicit universal approbation from the Norwegian-American Lutheran community. On the contrary, he often plunged into controversy. And it is not at all difficult to find widely differing estimates of the man by his contemporaries. Some of those who most strongly opposed him and his work described him as a demagogue, as one who grasped for power by practicing church politics, as one who spoke much of freedom while being unwilling to grant it to those who did not agree with him. Sverdrup's supporters, however, regarded him as a true champion of the Christian congregation, as an advocate of the genuine liberty belonging to the people of God, and as an able preacher, teacher, and writer. John O. Evjen has suggested that some followers of Sverdrup regarded his concept of the Christian congregation as the most profound interpretation since the time of the New Testament. Perhaps such varying opinions are inevitable when evaluating a person strongly committed to his principles.[3]

The term "American" has been applied to Georg Sverdrup in parts two and three of this study. The word has been used in a variety of ways in regard to immigrants. Some writers use it to indicate a person who has made a complete transition to the English language, while others imply that an American is one who has lost all distinctive features of Old World culture as he or she has become assimilated into that of the New World. Neither of these usages applies to Sverdrup. He continued to write and speak Norwegian throughout his life, although he could also use English; he also retained an appreciation of many facets of Norwegian culture despite his strong criticisms of what he felt were abuses in the state church. Sverdrup has here been called an American for another reason: his thinking reflected certain themes and motifs central to the American tradition. Among them are a commitment to freedom—religious and political—a defense of the separation of church and state as the best setting in which to build God's church, and a belief that the American mission included establishing the correct pattern for God's kingdom so that Christians in other nations could follow the example. Such views, which gave impetus and urgency to Sverdrup's activities, embody at least one aspect of what it means to be American.

PART I
THE EUROPEAN HERITAGE (1848–1874)

One

"The Norwegian Matrix"*

The nineteenth century was for Norway a period of an "awakening of storybook proportions and a marvelous period of expansion on all fronts," writes church historian Einar Molland. It was a time of ferment and activity that produced many changes in political and economic life, in literary expression, in education, and in religion. A new sense of national unity was created. "In all fields we see revolutionary developments and an unfolding of life which forms a sharp contrast with the preceding centuries."[1]

Georg Sverdrup was born almost in the middle of that period of change. He was born on December 16, 1848, in Balestrand, on the Sognefjord, one of the beautiful fjord areas of western Norway. During his first twenty-five years in Norway, he felt the influence of many of the currents and impulses that contributed to the social ferment and creativity of the time. Within the broader field of social and political change, the religious developments will be emphasized here, for it is primarily in that context that Georg Sverdrup's life may best be understood. Yet religious movements do not exist in isolation from other conditions. Many

---

*The chapter title is from Melvin A. Helland, trans., *The Heritage of Faith: Selections from the Writings of Georg Sverdrup* (Minneapolis, 1969), 9–35.

factors need to be considered in order to understand the man Sverdrup became.

NINETEENTH-CENTURY NORWAY

A good place to begin a discussion of nineteenth-century Norway is in 1814. It would be difficult to overestimate the significance of that year for the subsequent development of the country. Before that date Norway had been united with Denmark for more than 400 years. Copenhagen had been the seat of power, with Norway in many ways a province of the Danish kingdom. Government officials in Norway, many from Denmark, tended to form a class by themselves. Denmark made certain unfortunate political alliances during the Napoleonic Era, however, and one of the results was a treaty arrangement in 1814 that freed Norway from Danish control. Although Norway then entered into a personal union with Sweden, a country on the side of the victors at the Treaty of Kiel, nationalistic impulses were at work. Norwegians drafted a constitution for their country at Eidsvoll in 1814.[2]

The constitution, which has been described as the last liberal constitution in Europe growing out of the Revolutionary Era, proved to be of great importance to the Norwegian people. In it one can see ideas that are similar to those in the American constitution and in the French Enlightenment's statements on human freedom. During the time Norway was united with Sweden, the monarch generally agreed to rule in accordance with the provisions of the Norwegian constitution, giving the Norwegians a great deal of freedom in the conduct of their domestic political affairs. The problems inherent in such a union, however, led to its peaceful dissolution in 1905.

Examples of the flowering of the nationalistic spirit in Norway can be seen in some mid-nineteenth-century developments. The years 1844–1872 are called the age of national romanticism. Karen Larsen speaks of that period as a time when Norway "was developing a rich many-sided culture of its own, cosmopolitan-

European and yet markedly Norwegian in character."[3] It was a time of renewed self-awareness, with a concern for the enlightenment of the people. In order to establish and preserve a distinct national identity, efforts were made also to collect the folklore that had been handed down for generations. Linguists and writers also became interested in searching out a distinctively Norwegian language.

Yet Norway had a mostly rural society with a definite class structure. Most of the people were *bønder* (peasants), but there was also a distinct upper class composed of educated people, government officials, and the clergy. Landless tenant farmers comprised much of the lower class, along with servants and other workers. There was not much social intercourse between the classes. The gulf between the clergy and the *bønder*, for example, was difficult to bridge. The clergy were, after all, educated people as well as state officials. Often the lay people harbored a certain amount of suspicion of these representatives of the governing class. It was a barrier that was not easily overcome.

Resentment of class differences accompanied many Norwegians to America. Church historians E. Clifford Nelson and Eugene L. Fevold have written, for instance, that "the greatest grievance against his mother country that many a Norwegian emigrant to America carried in his heart was her tolerance of a social system which granted great privileges to the few and relegated the majority of her citizens to a position of social inferiority."[4] Georg Sverdrup was one who brought to America an awareness of this cleavage and an interpretation of its negative effects. Many of his efforts in this country were dedicated to the eradication of these effects, particularly as they manifested themselves in Norwegian-American religious life.

During the nineteenth century economic developments in Norway helped to improve the lot of many people, although many Norwegians also experienced hardship. Periodic depressions, at a time when families were large and opportunities limited, pre-

11

vented many from realizing their hopes for a secure future. Emigration seemed to offer the best alternative.

Economic factors, while primary, were not the only reasons for the exodus from Norway. Francis Sejerstad notes that the desire for greater religious freedom moved some to leave, and the American pattern of government also served as an attraction. Karen Larsen says that "all the discontent of the age — economic, religious, social, and political — sought release in emigration. It was but a phase of the revolt of the age against the old social system, and the restlessness and spirit of adventure natural in an age of transition developed into a veritable 'America fever'."[5] Beginning with a small group in 1825, hundreds of thousands of Norwegians left their homeland during the nineteenth and the early years of the twentieth centuries to improve their positions in life. The great majority of these people came to America.[6]

Professor Ingrid Semmingsen has stated that most Norwegian emigrants were working-class people in the broadest sense of that term. Speaking of the years 1866–1875, she finds few members of the official class, factory owners, or other owners of large businesses among them. More than nine-tenths of the emigrants from that time period belonged to "the simple class," as they have been called, and they were seldom rich. "The radicals of the time would perhaps have said that they were representatives of the People—with capital letters." The emigrants of succeeding years included a broader spectrum of social classes and occupations, but even then a large percentage of them were peasants and workers.[7] It was among these people that religious leaders such as Georg Sverdrup labored in America.

RELIGIOUS CURRENTS IN NINETEENTH-CENTURY NORWAY

Religious movements took place in this wider context. Christianity had, of course, been brought to Norway already in the tenth century, and during the Protestant Reformation in the early 1500s the country became Lutheran. In subsequent centuries

Norway felt the effects of such religious impulses as orthodoxy, pietism, and rationalism. Seventeenth-century Lutheran orthodoxy stressed the importance of correct doctrine and fostered a pattern of governmental authority over the church. Pietism accentuated the importance of personal religious experience and the propriety of lay people publicly bearing witness to their Christian faith. Rationalism, which emphasized the reasonableness of Christianity, tended to take a more optimistic view of human nature than that which was found in either orthodoxy or pietism. All three of these currents were part of Norway's religious mixture at the beginning of the nineteenth century.[8]

Although the constitution of 1814 and its amendments reflected in general a liberal spirit and outlook, it did call for the retention of Lutheranism as the official religion of the realm in such provisions as:

"Article Two: The Evangelical Lutheran religion shall remain the public religion of the state. Such inhabitants as profess this religion are required to educate their children therein.

"Article Four: The King shall always profess, maintain, and defend the Evangelical Lutheran religion.

"Article Sixteen: The King shall regulate all public religious and church service, all meetings and assemblies relating to religious matters, and shall see that the public teachers of religion follow the rules prescribed for their guidance."[9]

One church historian, in discussing the Norwegian constitution, notes that while many of the men at Eidsvoll favored the Enlightenment idea of religious freedom, within Norway they saw no religious minorities. Norway had a different history in this respect from America or France. In Norway the entire people formed one church and all the Eidsvoll men belonged to it. The framers of the constitution were thus faced with two conflicting interests: to promote the principle of religious freedom or to preserve the old pattern with a confessionally unified people and a sovereign church. The latter interest prevailed.[10] Andreas

Aarflot adds that what one sees in these statements in the constitution is a pattern in which the king is regarded as a Christian prince who holds the authority and control of the church. This approach follows the old Lutheran pattern in which the monarch combined religious and secular powers.[11]

Within the context of the Lutheran state church in Norway there are four nineteenth-century religious impulses that should be discussed as a background for an examination of Georg Sverdrup. Three of these movements — Haugeanism, the Johnsonian awakening, and the "church reform" movement — had a direct influence on his life and thought. The influence of the fourth — Grundtvigianism — is perhaps less obvious, but there are certain similarities and points of contact with Sverdrup's beliefs.

The Haugean movement takes its name from a peasant's son, Hans Nielsen Hauge (1771–1824), a lay evangelist who had a profound influence on the religious life of Norway. While working in his father's field in 1796, he felt a personal religious experience that convinced him that he must bear witness to Christianity among his people. For a number of years thereafter, Hauge traveled to many parts of Norway as a lay preacher, despite laws forbidding such activity. This—and the influence of his ideas—eventually led to his imprisonment, but even years of incarceration could not stop the movement that he had set in motion. The Haugean impulse set its mark on much of subsequent Norwegian Christianity.[12]

Haugeanism arrived on the scene at a time when rationalism was strong in clerical circles. Hauge and his followers, by their stress on the necessity for repentance and conversion, sought to call people back to what they considered to be a vital Christian experience. In many respects the Haugean movement, with its emphasis on a personally experienced Christianity, can be seen as a rebirth of some of the dictates associated with pietism. Some scholars of Lutheranism maintain, however, that the legalistic emphasis in Hauge's preaching and his outlook on civic involvement were not derived from that movement. The stress upon "obedience to God's law as an expression of vital faith" and the generally negative attitude of many Haugeans toward some of the worldly amusements, such as dancing and cardplaying, have led to the characterization of the Haugeans as the "Puritans of Norway." And it is true that in the Haugean perspective much emphasis was placed on the importance of the committed life and a break with the world.

Equally important, however, is the fact that Hauge urged his followers to remain within the existing Lutheran church. Haugeanism can be seen as an "example of conventicle Christianity within the framework of the Lutheran state church." That is, it stressed the importance of small groups gathering for mutual edification. The movement had an effect primarily on one class, the peasants, but it influenced not only the religious sphere but also the economic, political, and social life of the country.[13]

That Georg Sverdrup appreciated and was influenced by the Haugean movement becomes clear from his many references to it. He described it as a "true Christian awakening" and saw it as the source of much that was vital and significant in Norwegian and Norwegian-American church life.[14]

The second of the nineteenth-century Norwegian religious movements to be noted here is the Johnsonian awakening. Gisle Johnson (1822–1894) was a professor on the theological faculty of the university in Norway. He has been given a great deal of the credit for dealing a deathblow to theological rationalism in that country. An indication of the impact this man had on Norwegian theology and church life is reflected in Bishop J. C. Heuch's suggestion that the entire second half of nineteenth-century Norwegian church history ought to bear the title "Johnson's era" (*Johnsons tid*). Molland claimed further that in terms of "its broad effect upon Norwegian society and its significance for the ecclesiastical development in Norway," the Johnsonian awakening "undoubtedly surpasses the Hauge movement."[15]

Gisle Johnson began his career in 1849 and taught at the university until his death. He came to be recognized as a leading figure there, achieving his greatest distinction as a professor of systematic theology. He sought to be faithful to the Lutheran confessional writings, although his work also bore the imprint of certain nineteenth-century German and Danish thinkers.[16] One can see in Johnson's outlook a "combination of pietism and orthodoxy that has since been quite typical of Norwegian Lutheranism."[17]

Johnson was also instrumental in fostering a religious awakening among the clergy that helped to reconcile them to some degree with the Haugean movement. Johnson made a great impact on his students, and it was through these men—who eventually became pastors in the Norwegian church—that the renewal spread. Sverdrup, who had studied with Johnson, wrote an account of the Johnsonian awakening in which he spoke of the "unusual influence" of Johnson on the theological students. Sverdrup attributed the strength of the influence to the practice of Johnson and his colleague, Carl P. Caspari, of gathering with their students for devotional exercises on Saturday evenings. Sverdrup indicated that the devotions often made a deep impression on the assembled youthful minds.[18]

Sverdrup's general theological outlook and his comments about Johnson reflect his debt to this renewal movement. Sverdrup was, however, critical of what he considered to be Johnson's ambiguous position on lay witnessing. Johnson seemed to feel that the Augsburg Confession would permit lay witnessing in a congregation only in certain emergency situations, such as when the congregation had no pastor. Sverdrup's concept of the congregation led him to defend vigorously the right of the laity who had been equipped by the Spirit to make their witness publicly in the congregation.

The third religious development that needs to be discussed is the one known as the "church reform" movement. To understand this impulse it is necessary to refer again to the provisions

16

concerning religion in the constitution of 1814. These, it will be remembered, stated that the Lutheran religion was to remain the religion of the realm and gave to the king the power to regulate public religious functions. Andreas Seierstad has stated that this paragraph in the constitution makes clear that ecclesiastical authority was not to lie with the local congregation or in a hierarchy; it was to be gathered in the hands of the king.[19] Church affairs were placed in the hands of a governmental department, which was established near the end of 1814: "with that ecclesiastical self-government was out of the picture."[20]

Almost immediately there was dissatisfaction with that religious structure. Some of the men present at Eidsvoll in 1814, who had been influenced by Enlightenment thought, would have preferred a freer arrangement. On the other hand, some of the clergy desired a form that would vest control of the church in an ecclesiastical hierarchy. Then the Haugean movement released impulses that eventually caused the awakened laity to seek a greater voice in the control of church affairs. The agitation for reform was strong during much of the nineteenth century, with some members of the Sverdrup family taking a leading part in the movement.

Basically, the church reform movement was "the expression of a growing desire for a greater degree of independence on the part of the church as over against the state so that the church would have more freedom to regulate its own affairs."[21] Among the issues discussed were proposals calling for the abrogation of certain old laws that were seen as inhibiting lay activity, the establishment of a congregational council that would give the congregations more of a voice in their own affairs, the establishment of a type of church council (*kirkemøte*) that would have independent legislative authority for the church (though not the right of appropriations), and the elimination of laws that required confirmation and marriage in the church. Many of the political battles in Norway during the nineteenth century involved these issues in one way or another.[22]

Georg Sverdrup was deeply influenced by these struggles. He interpreted the church reform movement as one that was concerned with both religious liberty and the freedom of the congregation.[23] He brought with him to America these same concerns. One important distinction, however, needs to be kept in mind: many of the leaders in Norway were fighting for reform within the basic framework of the church. They stressed that they were not working for a church free from state connections.[24] Georg Sverdrup and his co-workers in America, on the other hand, found themselves in a place where their reformist efforts were devoted to building what they regarded as a genuinely free church and congregation.

Finally, brief mention will be made of the Grundtvigian movement and its influence in Norway. N. F. S. Grundtvig (1783–1872) was a Danish churchman and theologian who has been called "the greatest man in the church history of Denmark and the entire Northland." Reacting against the rationalism of Enlightenment thought and finding himself dissatisfied with the individualism of certain pietistic expressions of Christianity, he sought a more solid foundation for his Christian faith. This he believed he had found in his "matchless discovery," namely "the living word" of God, which Grundtvig maintained had been present in the church since its beginning. This living word was present most clearly, he believed, in the confession of faith in the baptismal service.[25]

Grundtvig was also determined to enlighten and elevate the common people. Deeply dissatisfied with the old classical pattern of education as it was embodied in the Latin schools, he called instead for the establishment of folk schools in which the people could be educated in their native language. Grundtvig believed that his countrymen could be brought to self-awareness through a study of Nordic literature and traditions rather than through a focus on classical antiquity. Many of his ideas spread to Norway, where some were enthusiastically received, but others en-

18

countered resistance. A number of the religious debates and controversies of the period revolved around Grundtvigian concepts.

It may be difficult to establish that Sverdrup was directly indebted to Grundtvig, since he dissociated himself from some Grundtvigian ideas, especially the concept of "the living word" as understood by the Danish churchman. Yet one finds in Sverdrup some of the same antipathy toward what he regarded as the tyranny of the educational pattern embodied in the Latin school. He also shared with Grundtvig a concern for the enlightenment and freedom of "the people."

The ferment taking place in Norway was part of the "awakening of storybook proportions" for which the century was known. These ideas were part of the intellectual baggage that Sverdrup brought with him to America.

THE SVERDRUP FAMILY

The Sverdrup family was one that made notable contributions to Norwegian national life. Some of its members have occupied eminent positions in political and religious affairs. Historian Halvdan Koht's comment reveals its status: "The Sverdrup family is one of those that has made a very deep imprint on the history of modern Norway. It stands alongside of such families as Wergeland, Stang, and Sars, and it is more versatile in its activities than the others."[26]

Students of the family have pointed to Denmark, where there is a village in South Jutland named Sverdrup, as the likely place to seek its roots. As early as the seventeenth century a member of this family, Peder Michelsen, was living in Norway. He and his wife established the line that produced a number of outstanding leaders, especially in the late eighteenth and nineteenth centuries.[27]

It is not the purpose of this study to recite the entire family tree. It is, however, useful to call attention to selected members of the Sverdrup line to give some indication of Georg Sverdrup's family milieu. If family tradition and heritage have something to do with shaping a person, it is reasonable to assume that the patterns of excellence and achievement established by some of the Sverdrups would make an impact on Georg.

The given name "Georg" appears repeatedly in the course of this family's history. One of those who bore this name, a great-uncle of the subject of this study, was a professor of classical languages at the university in Christiania. This earlier Georg Sverdrup (1770–1850) is also remembered as one of the leaders present at the historic Eidsvoll gathering in 1814, where he defended the principle of popular sovereignty. Ironically, he has been described as humanism's leading representative at the university, a spokesman for the classical tradition in education against which the later Georg argued so forcefully in America.[28]

Another member of the family who deserves to be mentioned here is Elisabeth Birgitte Sverdrup (1773–1865), an unmarried woman who exercised a strong influence on Johan Sverdrup, an influential uncle, and on Harald Ulrich Sverdrup, Georg's father. Quite early in her life she seems to have developed a hatred of despotism and oppression. Then, while living in Copenhagen for a number of years, she learned German, which opened the door to a broader European cultural life. Ideas associated with the Enlightenment and the spirit of the French Revolution made a lasting impact on her. A strong faith in humanity marked her perspective.[29]

The Sverdrup who had the greatest impact on Norwegian life was undoubtedly Johan (1816–1892), a major political figure who was a member of the Storting, the Norwegian parliament, and eventually formed the first parliamentary government in Norway. As a youth he received private instruction from his aunt, the well-educated Elisabeth Sverdrup. He also attended the university, where he seems to have been attracted to liberal ideas. As a political leader he championed liberal causes and was instru-

H. U. and Caroline (Suur) Sverdrup and their sons, all of whom studied theology: Jakob, Edvard, Georg, Harald, Hersleb (Courtesy George M. Sverdrup)

mental in the formation of Venstre (the Left), a political party reflecting that stance. Halvdan Koht has written a three-volume study of Johan Sverdrup in which he says that such slogans as "liberty, equality, and fraternity" permeated Sverdrup's perspective. As Johan saw it, the people had lived in bondage for centuries; he was determined to break the political and ecclesiastical controls that had oppressed them. Johan was at the height of his political career when Georg was a young man.[30]

Harald Ulrich Sverdrup (1813–1891) was Johan's brother and Georg's father. He too received instruction from Elisabeth Sverdrup at an early age, and she awakened in him an interest in liberal causes. He attended the university, taught briefly in Christiania at the Nissen Latin School, and became a pastor in the Lutheran church in Norway. He also took part in politics, serving for a time as a member of the Storting. Active in causes associated with the church reform movement, he also published catechetical

21

writings that were widely used in Norway; his theological stance was conservative.[31]

H. U. Sverdrup and his wife, Caroline Suur, were the parents of eight children, five boys and three girls. All of them came to be associated with the life and work of the church—the sons as pastors or teachers of future pastors and the daughters as wives of pastors. Georg was the second of the five sons.

The oldest son, Jakob Liv Rosted Sverdrup (1845–1899), had a close relationship with Georg. Like his father, Jakob labored in both the ecclesiastical and political spheres. Not only was he a pastor and bishop in Norway, he was also elected to the parliament and served in the ministry of church and education. He too fought for some of the causes associated with the church reform movement: for several years he helped edit *Ny Luthersk Kirketidende* (New Lutheran Church Times), a journal associated with the movement. Like his brother, he was stirred by the liberal nineteenth-century Italian statesman Camillo Cavour's slogan of "a free church in a free state" and worked for the achievement of such a goal within the Norwegian context. Georg's youngest brother, Johan Edvard (1861–1923), served as a teacher, pastor, and theological professor in Norway.[32]

Thus we see that Georg Sverdrup was born into a family with many members prominent in Norwegian life, a family with a liberal and democratic political tradition. Some members had demonstrated both leadership and willingness to do battle for the ideas and programs they felt were right. Georg Sverdrup, who possessed some of these same qualities, gave expression to them in an American setting, in the midst of his fellow immigrants from Norway.

Two

The Education Of A Professor

Carl H. Chrislock has observed that Georg Sverdrup came to champion an anti-elitist position within Norwegian-American Lutheranism, but Chrislock makes another point about the man: in taking this stance "Sverdrup was not compensating for any personal academic deficiencies. As both friend and adversary unreservedly recognized, he had an admirable command of the tools of scholarship. He was an acknowledged member of the Norwegian-American community's intellectual elite . . ."[1] The concern of this chapter is to elucidate the process by which Sverdrup came to possess that "admirable command" — the process that equipped him for his role as a professor of theology.

Georg's father was a Lutheran pastor at Balestrand in Sogn, western Norway, where Georg spent his boyhood years. His early education illustrates the pattern followed by the official class in Norway: a tutor instructed children in the home. Fredrik S. Schiørn (1830–1908) was Georg's tutor. Schiørn, who had studied for a year in Denmark, became a theological candidate and in 1859 an assistant to H. U. Sverdrup in the parish at Balestrand. Among his responsibilities was that of teaching the children of Pastor Sverdrup, and he is said to have found "great joy in his gifted pupils." Schiørn was also clearly a friend of the church reform movement, as can be seen in some of his articles and essays. He shared with the Sverdrups a feeling of frustration arising from the control of the church by the state and sought a greater measure of freedom and responsibility for the Christian congregation. His work was instrumental in bringing about a religious awakening in the area.[2] It was this man who was responsible for Georg's boyhood instruction. It was probably during his youth that the foundation for Georg's later "polemics against the State Church, against the aristocratic parsonage idealized by the peasants, against the established culture and education of the pastors and against their proud bearing like royal officials" was laid, for "state, school and church constituted important subjects in Sverdrup's parental home."[3]

At the age of fifteen years, Georg Sverdrup made his entrance

The parsonage in Balestrand, Norway, where Georg was raised
(Courtesy George M. Sverdrup)

Church in Balestrand where Georg's father, H. U. Sverdrup, served
(Courtesy George M. Sverdrup)

into the ranks of higher education. In 1863 he enrolled at Nissen's Latin School in Christiania. An institution designed for the few who would receive a higher education, the Latin school's basic curriculum consisted of a classical course with languages, literature, and history as the main subjects, along with studies in Christianity. The young person who could, on the basis of study at the Latin school, pass the examinations for the *artium* degree was then equipped to undertake studies at the university.[4]

Hartvig Nissen, for whom the Nissen Latin School was named, was an important figure in the reform of the Norwegian educational system. His role can best be seen in the debates about education that raged in Norway and other Scandinavian countries during the nineteenth century. These controversies can be brought into focus by referring to two words: *klassicisme* versus *realisme.* Proponents of *klassicisme* championed the pattern of education based on the classics and the study of languages. They maintained that an ideal world of values was made available to the student through the study of classical culture. For some the period of antiquity was seen as a golden age of the spirit, a time when there was a purer and more complete revelation of that which is truly human than at any other period. This meant that the Latin and Greek writings of antiquity were to form the staple of the educational diet, the means by which a student would become truly educated.

Those who spoke for *realisme* wanted to found *realskoler,* to make room for the new natural sciences that were coming to the fore during the nineteenth century and for courses that might be regarded as more practical in nature. Some who took this stance resented what they regarded as the tyranny of classical education, seeking a change to a more open educational system. From the 1830s to the 1850s supporters of these viewpoints struggled for dominance.[5]

Hartvig Nissen was involved in this conflict. As a young man he had studied in Denmark, where he had been influenced by, among others, Grundtvig, a vigorous exponent of change in educational methods. Grundtvig's view of the Latin schools, for example, was that they were "schools for death" because they were built upon an *ufolkelig* (undemocratic) foundation. That is, he felt that they were not rooted in "the people," but sought to impose an educational pattern that was foreign to them. Grundtvig advocated "schools for life" that would throw off the tyranny of Latin in order to give the national character, as expressed in the mother tongue and literature, an opportunity to develop to the fullest. This idea reflected not only *realisme,* but also democratic and nationalistic elements.[6]

In stressing the importance of a *folkelig* education, Grundtvig did not mean to imply that scholarly learning was of no value. He did feel, however, that it was necessary to form a link between scholarship and the popular education of the people. He thought the clergy should constitute this link.

In 1843 Nissen opened a school in Christiania to put some of Grundtvig's ideas into practice. The unique thing about this school was its attempt to be both a Latin school and a *realskole*—to combine the two educational patterns within the same institution. The curriculum was set up so that those students who were just beginning the school would take all classes together. A division would later be made between those who would follow the classical pattern and those who would follow the program of the *realskole*. The latter called for science courses and a more practical emphasis. Nissen's school was a bold departure from existing practice.[7]

Georg Sverdrup was not the first in his family to be associated with the school. His father taught religion and German there before he became a clergyman at Balestrand, and Georg's older brother, Jakob, had studied there before him.

Georg studied for two years at the Nissen school. Following the classical program, he took the *artium* (university entrance) examinations in August and September, 1865. He was examined in thirteen areas, including "mother tongue," Latin, Greek, Hebrew, German, French, and English, as well as religion, history, geography, arithmetic, and geometry. He scored a number one—the highest score—in all but two of these areas and received the overall grade of *laudabilis*, the highest score that one could receive on such examinations.[8]

Georg became a student at the university in Christiania (Det kongelige Frederiks universitet) in 1865. He later wrote that for the next six years he studied philosophy and theology, partly at Norway's national university and partly in Germany.[9] Scholars have not discovered where or how long he may have been in Germany, though a persistent tradition says that he studied for a year or more at Erlangen. This supposition cannot be substantiated by the records, although it seems clear that he visited

Germany for several months; during that time he may have attended a university.[10]

There is no doubt that he studied at the university in Christiania, which had been established in 1811. The 1860s and 1870s have been described as a "quiet and peaceful period" for the school, a time of steady and forceful inner development.[11] The records of the student society (*studentersamfundet*) from the 1860s indicate that many students gathered in the evenings to discuss such topics as pan-Scandinavianism in relation to the national movements, the merits of a classical education, Old Norse in the schools, politics, and the relationship between philosophy and Christianity. An example of this type of meeting was the gathering held in Christiania in 1869, which was also attended by students from the Swedish and Danish universities. Bjørnstjerne Bjørnson called for a movement in a new direction: away from the academic orientation and toward a popular one. Arguing that an effort should be made to build on a popular foundation, he declared that the university must be opened to all, whether they had passed the examination or not. In Bjørnson's thinking it was spirit rather than knowledge that fostered unity, which was his goal. And so he stressed that an exclusive emphasis on the academic (*studenteriet*) must be done away with so that that which is "of the people" (*det folkelige*) might take its place.[12] This brief look at the situation at the university when Georg Sverdrup was a student there reveals some of the topics and concerns that stirred the young people at that time. The records do not indicate the extent to which Georg involved himself in these discussions.

It is certain, however, that in September, 1866, Georg took the *examen philosophicum*, an examination given one year after the *artium*. The intervening year enabled the student to pursue general studies at the university level before beginning work within his chosen specialization. The university records indicate that Georg wrote a brilliant *examen philosophicum*. He was examined in eight areas (mathematics, natural history, Greek, Old Norse, history, physics, philosophy, and astronomy) and scored a number one in each; the overall evaluation given him was *laudabilis preceteris*, a designation reserved for outstanding achievement.[13]

Having completed this examination Georg could begin his work under the theological faculty at the university. The four professors there specialized in the Old Testament, the New Testament, church history, and systematic theology. The two who made the greatest impact on students were Gisle Johnson and Carl P. Caspari. As has been noted, Johnson became best known in the areas of systematic theology and the history of dogma. Caspari achieved distinction as an Old Testament specialist and gained an international reputation as a scholar of patristics, the study of the writings of the early church fathers. In purely scholarly terms he was by far the most noted figure on the faculty, having published many learned and technical works. A strict confessional Lutheran, he was a follower of the noted German conservative scholar E. W. Hengstenberg.[14]

Sverdrup's main area of interest as a student was in Old Testament studies. Several of his notebooks from Caspari's 1867–1868 lectures, which have been preserved, reflect both the professor's great learning and Sverdrup's introduction to the thinking of some of the leading men in the field. Another notebook, called "hebraiske gloser" (a type of Hebrew lexicon written out by Sverdrup), indicates that he possessed genuine linguistic talents.[15]

During his student days Georg also developed a lively interest in some of the church reform issues. This is evidenced in a series of five pamphlets published in 1869 and 1870 by Georg, his brother Jakob, and Georg Schielderup, young men speaking out on the issues of the day. They argued for reform of some existing practices and spoke out clearly and boldly for freedom in religious matters. The pamphlets dealt with such issues as the organization of the apostolic congregations, the status of the pastoral office in the church, religious and ecclesiastical freedom, the liberalization of the laws on confirmation, and the establishment of a congregational council. Georg Sverdrup, who was the youngest of the three, wrote on the liberalization of confirmation. He argued against the Norwegian laws that made the rite compulsory, laws that not only made it a prerequisite to admittance to the Lord's Supper but also to certain civil rights. Sverdrup maintained that the decision to be confirmed should be a completely free choice, because coerced faith was not in accord with biblical understanding. He saw in the elimination of laws requiring confirmation a two-fold freedom: for the individual to make a confession of what he believed, and for the congregation to let the word of God and only the word of God be the moving force behind the motivations of individuals. Sverdrup was a theological student in his early twenties when he wrote that pamphlet.[16]

By 1871 he was prepared to take his *theologisk embedsexamen*, a test that would determine whether he was qualified to hold a position in the church. The written papers from that examination give us some insights into Georg's capabilities and theological stance. Like the other students, he was assigned six topics: three were concerned with biblical issues; one was historical in nature; another had to do with systematic theology; and the last focused on ethics.[17]

The three biblical studies essays consisted of expositions of Psalm 90:1–8 and John 16:5–11, and a discussion of the authorship of the book of Hebrews. The first two demonstrate some of the linguistic and exegetical abilities of the young Sverdrup. They reveal a student with a good command of the biblical languages and with the ability to develop a careful, thorough exposition of the passages under consideration. His manner was forthright: he raised a question and proceeded directly to answer it. His outlook was basically conservative, and he made few references to specific commentators or interpreters. Sverdrup's essay on the authorship of Hebrews indicates his knowledge of the so-called critical questions in biblical studies. He noted the many names that had been put forward as possible authors of the letter, but felt it necessary to rely on internal evidence in this case. On the basis of cited pieces of evidence, Sverdrup rejected the position that Hebrews was written by Paul and stated that Luther's guess (Apollos, a Jewish convert to Christianity) might have been right. He did not insist on this view, however. Although in his teaching in America Sverdrup did not devote much time to the discussion of such issues in biblical studies, this essay shows that he was capable of doing so.

The essay on the history of the church and its dogma treated the history, doctrine, and effects of the heresy of Manichaeism through the Middle Ages. It appears to be a capable discussion, though Sverdrup did not write so confidently here as in his papers on biblical topics, systematic theology, or church-state issues.

The systematic theology paper discussed the doctrine of justification by faith. Sverdrup pointed to the centrality of this doctrine for the Lutheran church, taking a conservative stance: man is a sinner who stands under judgment; only God can save him. Christ has made salvation possible, and justification is based solely on what God has done in Christ. There is nothing in man that merits or contributes to his justification. Does that mean that all men are justified? Sverdrup's answer was no, for there is a condition required of man, and that is faith. This faith, created in man by the Word of God, is necessary for his salvation. The issue of justification by faith arose later in Sverdrup's life also, for it was one of many topics debated by Norwegian Lutherans in America.

The most useful essay, for the insights it gives into Sverdrup's later activities in America, is the one in the field of ethics, which discusses the church's relationship to the state. Sverdrup began this paper with a historical section. He pointed to three major epochs: the early period, in which the church had to fight for

31

its right to exist; the Middle Ages, in which there was an alliance between church and state, with the church seeking to dominate; and the Reformation, when the church fought for its freedom from the state and sought to give to the state the right to regard itself as appointed by God. The princes soon took control, however, and the Lutheran church became a state church—a church controlled by the secular power.[18]

Sverdrup then took up the issue of what the relationship between church and state should be. He discussed the nature of the church and the nature of the state. The church, he maintained, is a kingdom on earth rooted in faith and love. It demands freedom so that its members may freely confess their faith. This viewpoint also implies freedom and respect for other religious positions. Sverdrup declared that the principle of religious liberty was essential to the nature of the church. Christianity, he argued, bears religious liberty in its banners. The state, he said, is a natural kingdom, appointed by God, with its own task—the furtherance of justice and righteousness—to carry out. The state can and should encourage the church in its midst, for the church benefits the state by encouraging obedience.

Do these principles call for some sort of alliance between church and state? Sverdrup's response was no: an alliance would stand in opposition to religious liberty. He rejected the situation of a church that dominates the state (*kirkestaten*) as well as that of a state that dominates the church (*statskirken*). Maintaining that the principle of religious liberty demands the separation of church and state, he concluded that the state should deal with the church as a voluntary society (*fri forening*) in its midst. Cavour's phrase "the free church in the free state" expressed his idea of the proper relationship, and he felt that history was moving in that direction.

Sverdrup received the overall evaluation of *laudabilis* on his *embedsexamen* and was therefore in a position to take up work in the church. He did not do so immediately, however. For some

Wedding picture of Georg and Cathrine (Heiberg) Sverdrup
(Courtesy George M. Sverdrup)

eight years he had lived and studied in the intellectual atmosphere of Norway's leading city. He apparently decided to spend the next three years in further study, teaching, and travel. Describing his post-graduate activities, Sverdrup wrote that he "engaged in educational work at Christiania, continuing at the same time theological and linguistic studies" until he went to Paris in the spring of 1873.[19]

He had received a stipend enabling him to spend about six months studying in that city. The purpose of his study was to continue his work on the Semitic languages, notably Arabic and Assyrian, and to become familiar with the French scholarly literature dealing with historical studies of Israel. He also reported attending lectures on the Koran and on the Assyrian cuneiform inscriptions. Having received permission to study in the Bibliotheque nationale, he had access to a rich collection of books. He took the opportunity to read a number of works about the Arab peoples by French and German scholars.[20]

In addition to scholarly journeys, Sverdrup traveled in Italy and England. In 1880 he wrote an essay on "The Congregation in the Catacombs" in which he discussed the meaning and significance of the catacombs around Rome. It seems likely that this essay grew out of impressions gained during his travels. In England he is known to have preached at the Seaman's Church in a place called North Shields.[21]

1874 was in many respects a year of change for Georg Sverdrup. Not only did he marry Cathrine Elisabeth Heiberg on June 25 of that year, but he also received and accepted a call to become a theological professor at Augsburg Seminary in Minneapolis. He would be making a transition from the Old World to the New World. Following the accepted educational pattern in Norway, Sverdrup had shown himself to be a very capable student and had availed himself of opportunities for advanced study and travel. There is even an unsubstantiated report that some Norwegians considered him a prospective candidate for a professorship at the university in Christiania.[22]

But Georg Sverdrup had been influenced by educational reforms that were being debated in Europe. He had been stirred by the impulses flowing from the Haugean movement, the Johnsonian awakening, and the church reform movement. America would provide the context in which Sverdrup would seek to realize his ideas about church life, the education of pastors, and the Christian congregation.

PART TWO
AMERICAN EDUCATOR, THEOLOGIAN,
CHURCHMAN: FORMATIVE YEARS (1874–1890)

Three

Augsburg Seminary: Professor and President

Georg Sverdrup emigrated to America in 1874 in response to the call from Augsburg Seminary. He arrived in Minneapolis on August 17.[1]

How should we characterize the America to which Sverdrup came? Any good textbook in American history can provide the broad outlines of an answer. One such text describes the last three decades of the nineteenth century as "years of contrast and contradiction." It goes on to say that the "age was at once dynamic and unchanging, certain and confused, vulgar and genteel, imitative and original . . . Mark Twain called the period 'the gilded age,' and it was indeed a shoddy alloy of precious and base—cheap, shiny, tasteless." That same book points to the rapid pace of change by noting that "in 1870 . . . buffalo still roamed the plains; Minneapolis had only about 13,000 inhabitants; few Americans knew where Samoa was; and Andrew Carnegie had not yet devoted himself to the steel business. By 1900 . . . buffalo were protected in zoos; Minneapolis was a thriving city of more than 200,000; Americans had governed part of Samoa for a dozen years; and Andrew Carnegie was about ready to sell his steel business for several hundred million dollars."[2]

In short, it was to post-Civil War America that Sverdrup came.

39

1874 was near the end of Reconstruction in the South and in the midst of the political scandals and corruption associated with the Grant administration. The post-Civil War period was the time of an industrial transformation associated with the expansion of the railroads, the growth of steel and petroleum empires, and the emergence of industrial leaders who have been called "robber barons" by some later historians. Intellectuals were feeling the impact of evolutionary thought, which was applied in a number of areas, including business and the social sphere. This was an era too that saw the rapid growth of cities and the continued westward expansion of the nation, as well as the passing of the frontier that historian Frederick Jackson Turner was later to identify as so vital to American history. Immigration continued to transform American society. There were literally millions of immigrants—some have said as many as 45 millions during the nineteenth century—who left their homelands and sought a new destiny in the New World. The America of the last decades of the nineteenth century was a place of change and movement.

Perhaps all of this needs to be kept in some perspective as far as our consideration of Georg Sverdrup is concerned. It cannot be claimed that he came to the very center of intellectual ferment or industrial change. Minnesota, after all, had only become a state in 1858—less than twenty years before Sverdrup's arrival. Much of the state retained some of the characteristics of a frontier region. Yet it is clear that many of the forces that were shaping modern America were at work there.

And the Upper Midwest — including Minnesota — had a distiction of its own: it was a region where many Scandinavian immigrants had settled. The Scandinavian immigration was, of course, only a part of the larger movement to American shores. The Norwegians in turn made up only a part, though a major part, of that immigration.

The year 1825 marks the beginning of Norwegian group migration to America. Historian Carlton Qualey has stated that in the period 1825–1915, Norwegian immigrants to the United States numbered 754,561. Although small in comparison with the numbers who came from some of the larger countries, it is high in terms of the percentage of Norway's total population. The United States Immigration Commission reported that between 1820 and 1910, "Norway has sent a larger percent of its population to America than any other country excepting Ireland."[3] A goodly number of them came to Minneapolis and surrounding areas. Georg Sverdrup's activities took place within a Norwegian-American environment.

By the time of Sverdrup's arrival the Norwegian Lutherans in this country had organized themselves into no less than four (it was soon to be five) church bodies. Attention has been called to the varying and sometimes conflicting trends that appeared within the church in Norway during the nineteenth century. For the most part these tendencies were contained within the state church there, but in America the religious situation was different. The new-found liberty in spiritual matters allowed the removal of Old World restraints. "Sprouts of disagreement . . . found a good soil . . . and developed in all their power."[4] The initial result was a fragmentation of those Norwegian Americans who joined Lutheran congregations, leading to the formation of separate synods and groups and to much controversy among them.

The Evangelical Lutheran Church in America (Den evangelisk lutherske kirke), formed in 1846 and commonly known as Eielsen's Synod, was the earliest expression of the low-church tendency among the immigrants. Its founder was Elling Eielsen, lay preacher and pastor, who came to America in 1839 and worked among Norwegian immigrants until his death in 1883. This synod strove to realize his emphasis on an experienced religion and sought to resist formalism and what it considered to be "mass Christianity." In 1876 the group split and a faction known as Hauge's Synod emerged as a second body, seeking to give expression to some of the themes that had been associated with the Haugean movement in Norway.[5]

Very different were the concerns of the high-church Norwegian

Evangelical Lutheran Church in America (Den norske evangelisk lutherske kirke i Amerika), commonly called the Norwegian Synod. This group, formed in 1853 and led by a group of able, university-educated pastors, emphasized pure doctrine and valued a more formal type of worship service. Quite early in its history this church body established contacts and developed a working relationship with the Missouri Synod, a Lutheran church of German background. This relationship strengthened the insistence of the Norwegian Synod on pure doctrine. In the 1880s the synod was torn by a doctrinal controversy over predestination, and a group known as the Anti-Missourian Brotherhood withdrew from it.

There were also Norwegian Lutherans in America who were not satisfied with the directions of either the low-church or the high-church group. Some of these people found a church home in 1860 with Lutheran immigrants of Swedish background in a group generally called the Augustana Synod. Its official name was the Scandinavian Evangelical Lutheran Augustana Synod (Den skandinaviske augustana synode). In 1870 the Norwegians decided to make a peaceful separation from the Swedes in order to form their own church body, but differences and misunderstandings led to an unexpected result: instead of one new Norwegian-background church body there came to be two. Formed in 1870, these were the Norwegian-Danish Augustana Synod (Den norske augustana synode) and the Conference for the Norwegian-Danish Evangelical Lutheran Church in America (Norsk-danske konferentse), commonly called the Conference. Both sought to occupy a position between low-church and high-church tendencies.

Sverdrup became a member of the Conference when he came to America. He said later of this body that it took a central position between two extremes: that of stressing the individual as a believer to the neglect of the congregation, on the one hand, and that of elevating the pastor to a position of dominance, on the other. The Conference, Sverdrup maintained, emphasized the significance of the congregation. In his short response at the welcoming program eight days after his arrival in Minneapolis, Sverdrup gave additional insight into his attitude toward the Conference. He spoke of leaving fatherland, family, and friends because of the spiritual need among his countrymen in America. He spoke of the dangers that immigrants faced: the temptations of the lust for money and of the different teachings that could tear people away from the faith. In addition, he said, there were few who could serve as guides, teachers, pastors, and shepherds for them, and strife existed among the churches established here. Sverdrup expressed his conviction that the Conference had seen clearly the right remedy for the situation by showing the will and the ability to train its own spiritual leaders.[6]

Augsburg Seminary and its related academy were founded in 1869 in Marshall, Wisconsin. In 1872 the seminary moved to Minneapolis, where the Conference maintained it primarily to prepare pastors to serve that church body. Supporters of the school were proud of its status as "the first Norwegian seminary in America."[7]

Sverdrup was not a founder of Augsburg Seminary, however. That honor belongs to August Weenaas, the school's first president and from 1869 to 1873 its sole theological professor. That energetic and hard-working man sought to develop and carry on a respectable program of education. In those earliest years the institution was divided into two parts: a preparatory department (*forberedelsesafdeling*) and a theological department (*theologisk afdeling*). The preparatory department, which offered a two-year program, attempted to equip students for studies in the seminary. The theological department offered basic courses in the Old Testament, the New Testament, dogmatics, church history, and practical theology. Weenaas served as the instructor in the theological department, while an assistant and some of the abler theology students taught the courses in the preparatory department.[8]

Several years later the faculty of Augsburg Seminary was increased. Sven Oftedal arrived in 1873. Oftedal (1844–1911), born and educated in Norway, was a gregarious, outgoing person with real gifts as a linguist. He served as a professor at the seminary from 1873 to 1904, teaching mainly church history and the New Testament. He and Sverdrup came to be leading figures at Augsburg during their years of association with the school. The two men were quite different in temperament, but their views concerning the church, theological education, and freedom of religion were much the same, and they were lifelong friends.[9]

When Conference officials were recruiting him for the position at Augsburg, Oftedal had told them that two other well-trained, able young men would be open to calls as professors if they were needed. The two, Georg Sverdrup and Sven Rud Gunnersen, joined the staff as professors in 1874, bringing the faculty total to four. Gunnersen taught primarily church history. This increase in teaching personnel meant that a division of labor could be effected in accordance with the specialities and interests of the four professors. Church historian J. A. Bergh later wrote that in this faculty of four talented men lay both the strength and the weakness of the Conference. As a group they were exceptionally able, but they also took some stands that polarized the Conference. The staff did not remain intact very long, however, as Weenaas returned to Norway in 1876 and Gunnersen left Augsburg in 1883.[10]

Writing some years later, Weenaas, who eventually came to feel somewhat pushed aside by his younger colleagues, characterized the three young men who had become friends in Europe and who joined the Augsburg faculty in 1873 and 1874. Sverdrup at once gave the impression of being the leader of the group, said Weenaas, adding: "he [Sverdrup] was the *mind*, while Gunnersen was the *heart* and Oftedal the *spirit* in the new triumvirate."[11]

The expansion of the faculty also permitted further development of the program at Augsburg. In 1874 the Seminary's board of directors put forward a proposal calling for an expansion of the program. Weenaas felt this was necessary in order to prepare students better for theological study, and to meet a deeply felt need for "an educational institution that could spread enlightenment and general education among the Norwegian people in America." To attain these goals the board of directors submitted its proposal for both expansion and an altered plan of instruction to the annual meeting of the church body.

The plan called for an expanded preparatory school with a one-year common class (*fællesklasse*) for all entering students who did not have the necessary background for taking up work in the more advanced classes, and units of a more advanced nature, described by Chrislock in his history of the institution as college-level departments. One of these, the Greek department, later became a four-year course whose primary purpose was to prepare students for the three-year theological program. The complete plan for the Greek department envisioned courses in Norwegian, English, history, religion, geography, Greek, Latin, and German.[12]

The parallel college-level course of study, taking a leaf from the book of Nissen's Latin School, was the department of practical studies (*realafdeling*), "which seeks to impart the knowledge that the practical life demands of an educated man." This four-year sequence was to offer courses for those students who did not plan to enter the ministry. The program for this department included some of the same subjects as those taken in the Greek department (Norwegian, English, history, geography, and religion), but instead of Greek, Latin, and German, it called for instruction in mathematics, bookkeeping, Old Norse, physical geography, natural science, and American government.

The most advanced level in the school was the theological department, a three-year program that would help to equip a man to serve as a pastor. In addition to the courses they offered in this department, the professors were to teach in the preparatory school.

The entire faculty also expressed itself on the topic of the new program for Augsburg Seminary, issuing a statement entitled "A Program for Augsburg Seminary and Its College Departments, Adopted by the Board of Directors on August 31, 1874, Together with an Interpretative Statement by the Faculty."[13] This document, the result of the joint efforts of the four theological professors, interpreted the new program that was being proposed for the seminary and made explicit its underlying philosophy. The statement is marked by its writers' wish to develop a system of studies that would avoid spiritual tyranny and the deadening effects of a one-sided emphasis upon pure doctrine.

This "Program for Augsburg Seminary" contains interpretive comments about both college-level departments and the theological courses. Sverdrup may well have written the comments about the Greek department, which in their variance from traditional educational patterns indicate the development of something unique at Augsburg. They stress the importance both of cultivating an appreciation for the Norwegian heritage and of preparing students to enter into the mainstream of American life. They also emphasize the belief that students needed both a sound general education and skill in the languages necessary for further study.

The statement underscores the idea that a true education (*aandsdannelse*) consists of a personal search for the truth to the extent that it becomes a power decisive in thought and will, speech and action. Religion and history were thus regarded as the proper instruments of education. The selection of languages was on the basis of practical considerations—to facilitate the study of theology. "In principle," the program noted, "we are not humanists." There was no desire to have students learn classical culture as an end in itself. And so even the name of the department was to be different: instead of the old term "Latin School," it was to be called the "Greek Department" (*græskskole*). The point was that Greek is more useful than Latin for the study

Augsburg faculty in 1875, reflecting expansions of 1874 Plan
(Courtesy Augsburg College Archives)

of theology and that Greek, more than Latin, was the cultural language of the ancient world.[14]

The faculty's comments about the practical studies department reflect the desire for Augsburg Seminary to become a cultural focal point for Norwegians in America. To realize this goal, the department—constructed upon the same foundations as the seminary itself—would be of great importance. The document recognizes that only a relatively few persons would feel called to the ministry and that, if Augsburg's principles were carried to the people only by pastors, religious tyranny would become a possibility. It continues: "Our holy task must necessarily concern all who do not consider their Norwegian origin a disgrace

47

and who are not ashamed to contribute their national gifts to the great American development." Reflected here is a desire to reach "the farmer, the laborer, and the businessman," to convey "a liberal cultural outlook," and to educate people so that they will become "genuinely Christian citizens."

The professors' discussion of the three-year theological course indicates an attempt to develop a program that would educate pastors to be mature, authoritative, and independent spokesmen for the truth. It repeatedly stressed the dangers of a formalistic, rationalistic approach to theology. The goal of theological education was not to clutter the minds of students with citations, glosses, interpretations, or hairsplitting distinctions; rather it was to lead them to a greater understanding of Jesus Christ, the heart and center of God's Word. The purpose of theological education was to develop a personal, living conviction about religious truth, a way of coming to see more clearly how God works. To that end the courses offered were to be arranged in a series of three cycles that together formed an organic whole. A focus on Scripture, rather than on an orthodox dogmatic system, was to be the heart of the program. This point was underscored by the statement that "Christianity is history, because Christ is a historical person. Christianity's book—the New Testament—is history, because its writings contain an organic complex of facts, of events in His life, and His Word." In the comments concerning systematic theology the document underscored the idea that there was no greater danger for a theological student than to lose himself in a "dry rationalistic formalism." Such an approach, it was maintained, led the student into the danger of changing faith to reason and life to a form, a category, a correct doctrine. There "is a higher logic than the Aristotelian," they argued; "we know of another proof than the mathematical; we know of a higher truth than the reasonable 'pure doctrine,' namely, a conviction of faith that cannot be demonstrated and does not fit at all in the usual thought forms and logical categories . . . . dogmatics is not scientific knowledge but something higher, a knowledge of life which has its point of departure in the purely absurd or, what is the same thing, the highest truth: the Word became flesh."

In 1875 Georg's older brother, Jakob, wrote a sympathetic evaluation of the Augsburg faculty plan. In it he stated that those men proceeded from the fundamental principle that Christianity is a "living organism" in which all of God's gracious dealings are a revelation of a divine deliberation, every element of which is linked together harmoniously and inspired by one fundamental thought. Christianity, he continued, has come into the world through a historical process and it must be presented as a living organism. He indicated that while the Bible and biblical theology were central in the Augsburg plan, the professors there did not regard the Scripture as being simply a collection of passages to be commented on chapter and verse, supported by grammatical references, citations, and parallel passages. We have here, said Jakob Sverdrup, "an attempt at an organic concentration of the theological material with constant regard to Christianity's inner unity." This approach was quite different from what he had observed in European universities.[15]

The proposals were adopted, not only by Augsburg's board of directors, but by the Conference's annual convention as well. An attempt was made in the years following 1874 to implement them. In 1875 Georg Sverdrup, who was then secretary of the Augsburg faculty, spoke of the plan as a way to facilitate "interaction between the congregation and scientific knowledge (*videnskaben*), which we regard as a fundamental condition for a churchly development and to which only the free church gives opportunity in full measure." In his last report to the Conference as president of the seminary in 1876, Weenaas pointed to the plan with pride: "The task our school has undertaken is not that of giving the students a little taste of everything—which all too often seems to be the situation with the American schools—but of educating, by means of a coherent, principled plan of instruction, mature and independent-minded men who will be an asset to church and state."[16]

Although the Augsburg faculty thought it had developed something unique in the field of theological education, several features of its program were not without precedent. Like Norway during the nineteenth century, America too was the scene of vigorous debates about the nature of higher education. The basic pattern that had been established in the Colonial period, which continued well into the nineteenth century, was "the classical tradition" brought over from Europe. The prescribed course of study followed the same basic outline: its "foundation was the ancient classics and mathematics, on top of which came a thin layer of science and a thick topping of philosophy and ethics."[17]

At least as early as the 1820s critics challenged this pattern. And even though Yale University issued its famous report of 1828 in defense of the ancient languages and mathematics as "best suited to discipline the faculties," the debate continued. By the post-Civil War period Charles W. Eliot of Harvard and others began to argue for a revision of the traditional curriculum to serve the needs of the modern age. The new outlook found vigorous expression in the address Charles Francis Adams gave at Harvard in 1883. Adams, who had graduated from the college twenty-seven years earlier, was highly critical of the curriculum that had compelled the students to devote the best part of their school lives "to acquiring a confessedly superficial knowledge of two dead languages," an approach that regarded Greek and Latin as "the basis of all liberal education." Adams claimed that he merely wished to ask for recognition of a modern approach, a broadening of the basis of liberal education. The Augsburg professors were not alone, then, in their attack on the older system of education associated with the Latin school.[18]

The Augsburg Seminary proposals must also be seen in the context of the conflict among Norwegian Lutherans in America. The Augsburg men were particularly conscious of the disagreements between their group and the Norwegian Synod. As early as 1861 the latter body had established Luther College in Decorah, Iowa, to educate its clergy.

Luther College was not a seminary, but a theological preparatory school. Karen Larsen, who has written a study of her father, Laur. Larsen, the first president of that school, notes that Norwegian Synod ministers believed that the proper basis for studying theology "was a thorough classical course, and they were determined that as far as possible they would maintain the standards under which they themselves had been trained [in Norway]." Laur. Larsen made a strong case for tradition in a series of articles he wrote in 1868. In them he devoted the most space "to a defense of the classical course, presenting with conviction and force all the arguments of the humanists, and quoting Luther liberally." He also wrote dramatically of the desire of those associated with Luther College to give their educational program "a true classical foundation . . . for without it our 'civilized' age would soon sink into barbarism."[19] The Augsburg professors, on the other hand, felt that a new pattern of theological education was required to meet the needs of the free congregations in the New World.

What then was the fate of the Augsburg plan? How was it implemented? Chrislock has addressed this question directly: "Although the broad frame of reference running through the 1874 program would guide Augsburg's educational policy for many decades, only part of the blueprint became operative. Development of the beginning preparatory and Greek departments followed the program's specifications, but the department of practical studies never got underway, nor was Old Norse introduced. Augsburg also failed to become a major Norwegian-American cultural center guiding a moderately paced immigrant assimilation into American life. Instead, for more than four decades the institution remained essentially what it set out to be in 1869: a divinity school serving a minority wing of Norwegian-American Lutheranism."[20]

August Weenaas' last two reports to the annual conventions

of the Conference (1875 and 1876) before he resigned as president indicate that an initial attempt was made to implement the plan as completely as possible. He reported that in the preparatory department all three divisions were functioning: the common preparatory class, the Greek department, and the practical studies department. If so, they did not function long. Georg Sverdrup was elected Weenaas' successor in 1876. He occupied that position for the next thirty-one years. Despite Sverdrup's recommendations to the contrary, based on economic as well as theological considerations, the Conference elected B. B. Gjeldaker to take Weenaas' place on the faculty.

Sverdrup's first report to the annual convention of the Conference, made in 1877, related Augsburg's unique program to its sponsoring church body. The Conference, said Sverdrup, was recognized as the group that had "the national seminary." The motto of the school—"the Word became flesh"—reflected the conviction that what would truly gather the Norwegian people together was not an emphasis on pure doctrine or the holy life but the preaching of God's Word in its truth and purity in the language of the people.[21]

The reports of 1877 and 1878 also contained a brief summary of the courses taught during those school years; they made no reference to the practical studies department. By 1879 Sverdrup observed that after much difficulty and many disappointments, the Greek department finally had all four classes in operation. He added that the school had thus passed through the time of transition that had begun in 1874, since Augsburg had apparently abandoned the part of the plan calling for practical studies. In 1884 Sverdrup's statements made plain a change in direction: the institution, he wrote, should move toward becoming exclusively a divinity school. The record does not reveal the reasons for the change; possibly the combination of financial factors and Sverdrup's conviction that the pressing need for pastors dictated a concentration of resources in that area made the difference. In any case, the church body concurred with his opinion.[22]

In the years immediately following the adoption of the 1874 plan some people criticized it because the increased number of years of schooling would mean a shortage of pastoral candidates at a time when there was a great need for them in the church. The Augsburg staff argued that this was an inevitable but temporary result of upgrading theological preparation. The long-range result would be ministers who were better qualified to build America's free congregations.

Augsburg functioned for several years with three theological professors after Gjeldaker left in 1878, just two years after his arrival. The number was reduced to two in 1883, when Sven Gunnersen resigned, stating that the teachers did not work well together. For the next seven years Sverdrup and Sven Oftedal harmoniously promoted and defended the educational programs of the institution.

Consolidation was also taking place in the preparatory departments. In the school's early years the theological professors and various temporary instructors had taught classes in the common preparatory and Greek departments. Some of the more able students occasionally assisted them. In the 1880s, however, there was an effort to strengthen the college by electing full-time permanent teachers. Men such as John T. Bugge, John H. Blegen, Theodor S. Reimestad, Wilhelm M. Pettersen, and A. M. Hove joined the staff. Most of them had graduated from the Augsburg Greek department; several had also completed the theological course there and had served as pastors. One historian described all of these men as "able teachers . . . [who] worked well together." It seems clear that Sverdrup and his colleagues intended to build a school staffed at every level by like-minded people committed to their goals.[23]

Sverdrup also faced the practical problems that plague all school administrators. One early difficulty was lack of space. To alleviate it he urged the Conference congregations to consider setting up "folk high schools" (folkehøiskoler) in their settlements. These institutions, patterned after the Norwegian folk high schools that had grown out of Grundtvig's concern to enlighten the people, were to have a two-year course of study. Sverdrup believed that they could facilitate the transition from common schools to Augsburg's Greek department, thus making possible the elimination of the preparatory class. Although this recommendation was accepted by the Conference and approved at its annual meeting, the schools never materialized.[24] The lack of space continued to be a problem.

A more persistent problem was shortage of money. Sverdrup was connected with "the financial side of the work" at Augsburg in several ways. As early as 1874 he accompanied Weenaas on a trip through southern Minnesota and northern Iowa to solicit building funds. That fall he was appointed treasurer of the tuition fund of the school; he kept its accounts for several years. He also served as treasurer of the building committee in 1876–1877 and in 1886 was named chairman of a committee to solicit subscriptions for an endowment fund.[25]

Over the years Sverdrup wrote a number of editorials and articles about Augsburg's finances.[26] All of them reflect his concern that the school be established on a solid financial basis so that it might fulfill its calling, which he related to that of the larger church body: to build a free congregation to be Christ's witness in the world. It was essential to have a good seminary to prepare appropriately the pastors who would undertake this great task. Sverdrup was convinced that only an earnest and thorough education could prepare men to meet the great challenges of the pastorate. Repeatedly he urged the congregations to consider the great benefits they would get from such a seminary. They in turn should support the school, he argued, so that it would not have to remain in debt.

Sverdrup wrote often about the advantages of a permanent endowment fund. Many congregations made yearly donations to the seminary, but this often left the school in a rather difficult position: frequently the contributions did not cover the expenses. It also made it easy for disgruntled pastors or congregations to withhold their support. Sverdrup maintained that a permanent fund should be established so that those at the school could devote themselves to their proper tasks rather than continually worrying about the school's funding. The drive for an endowment would bear spiritual fruits, Sverdrup claimed, making the congregations more conscious of their role, strengthening the bonds in the church body, and contributing to church unity. He quoted with approval the statement that the Conference stands or falls with its seminary, believing wholeheartedly that it would be a great tragedy if it fell. He reiterated that he would do all in his power to sustain the school spiritually if the congregations would sustain it financially. The 1880s drive for an endowment fund raised a considerable amount of money, but accumulated debts and ongoing expenses meant that Augsburg faculty would need to continue their efforts to raise money to support their work.

Augsburg was never a large school during the years of Sverdrup's presidency. Between 1876 and 1907 the number of students in all three departments reached 201 only once. Most of the time the number fell between 100 and 200. The theological department was usually the smallest of the three. One year (1890–1891, a year of church union) the number enrolled in that course was 72, but it usually varied from 15 to 45.[27]

In addition to his presidential duties, Sverdrup also served as a professor. Although he instructed theological classes, he also taught in the preparatory and college departments. At the seminary level his courses varied with the number of professors — from two to five — on the faculty. He invariably taught the Old Testament, however, and often dogmatics as well. Other occasional duties included lectures on the New Testament books of Matthew, Hebrews, and James, as well as courses in symbolics and pastoral theology. At the college and preparatory levels he sometimes offered courses in religion, Greek, and French. His basic language of instruction was Norwegian, but he taught some of his lower-level classes in English. Sverdrup was also concerned about providing English instruction in the theological department. He argued that if pastors were to be prepared to enter genuinely into the life of this country and to lead the people to make their proper contribution to its development, it was essential that ministerial education include adequate training in the English language.[28] In this, as in some other areas, Sverdrup was a leader: the language question became a major issue among Norwegian Lutherans later in the nineteenth century.

John Evjen wrote that Sverdrup "showed most favorably his talent as a teacher when he lectured on Dogmatics." Evjen, who heard those lectures in the 1890s, added that "it cannot be said that Sverdrup presented many original thoughts. His material was essentially eclectic if one disregards his conception of the congregation. Furthermore, it cannot be said that he led the students to independent study of systematic theology." But Sverdrup's lectures held the interest of the students and, "when compared with those of the best Lutheran dogmaticians in America," had "the great advantage that they built on the Scriptures and did not stand in the service of the seventeenth century Theology or of the Concordia formula."[29] The next chapter will deal more fully with Sverdrup's general theological perspective.

Evjen's comments point up one of Sverdrup's leading characteristics as a teacher: he went his own way rather than depending on the views of others. Certainly he sought to be faithful to the Lutheran understanding of Christianity, believing that it offered the clearest presentation of the Gospel. He expressed his independence by building his dogmatics on the Scriptures rather than on the systems of other thinkers.

Georg Sverdrup was an effective teacher. He was not theatrical or dramatic, but his clear, earnest presentations made a lasting impression on many of his students. J. A. Bergh, who at times opposed some of the views and activities that Sverdrup championed, wrote in 1914 that as a teacher Sverdrup "has probably even yet had no superior among our people in America."[30]

Four

"New-Direction" Theologian

The "seemingly endless theological debates and bitter controversies" that went on among the Norwegian Lutherans in America between 1860 and 1890 have been called "theological warfare."[1] Differing emphases that had existed under one roof in the state church in Norway were brought over to the New World, where the differences were strengthened and even exaggerated. Much of the writing in church papers and theological journals and many of the discussions at synodical conventions and theological conferences reflected the divisions. Georg Sverdrup was an active participant in many of the debates, but in order to place him correctly in this context, it is necessary to discuss developments in America prior to his arrival.

The two church groups that had emerged in the earlier years of Norwegian immigration—Eielsen's Synod and the Norwegian Synod—represented different styles and concerns, as has been noted. Eielsen's Synod—and later the Hauge's Synod—embodied some of the revival impulses from Norway, especially those associated with Hans Nielsen Hauge. Its accent was on conversion and the new life in Christ. It rejected formalism in worship and what it regarded as mass Christianity, often harboring a suspicion of the type of clergy found in Norway. The Christian individual was its focus.

The Norwegian Synod, on the other hand, was characterized by a strong emphasis on pure doctrine, church order, and as much faithfulness to traditional forms as was possible in the new setting. Its relationship with the Missouri Synod strengthened the emphasis on pure doctrine and the feeling that it was necessary to resist those who had not preserved the true faith. It insisted on complete doctrinal agreement before there could be union and encouraged the holding of free conferences where doctrinal issues could be discussed and debated. The rapidly growing Norwegian Synod was for a number of years the numerically dominant group among Norwegian Lutherans in America.

The emergence of the Norwegian Augustana Synod and the Conference in 1870 made alternatives available to the two extremes represented by the earlier groups. While those who occupied this middle ground generally felt that the position of the Eielsen group was inadequate, their main energies were directed against the well-organized and articulate leaders in the Norwegian Synod.

Sverdrup's own theological approach drew on the confessional theology of the Erlangen school, which "aimed at a healthy synthesis of the Lutheran heritage with the new learning" of the nineteenth century. Those who subscribed to that view stressed the role of Christian experience in the development of a theological system. They also understood the role of Scripture differently from nineteenth-century repristination theologians who opposed rationalism and were committed to the outlook of seventeenth-century Lutheran orthodoxy. In one statement about the books of the Old Testament, for example, Sverdrup spoke of that canon as "the complete, inspired, written presentation of the divine salvation-revelation in the time of the old covenant. This divine revelation is essentially a holy history, governed by God's law and promise, a gracious guidance of a chosen people." Scripture presents, in this view, completely and infallibly, the divine revelation in the period of the Old Testament. "The coming into existence of Scripture follows revelation or holy history exactly, step by step." Therefore, one of the first tasks of an introduction to the Scripture was to sketch this holy history and to show where the various canonical books fit into it. Sverdrup drew a distinction between revelation and Scripture. Revelation as he defined it consisted of God's deeds. Scripture, on the other hand, was the complete, inspired, written presentation (*fremstilling*) of that revelation.[2]

Sverdrup's discussions of the biblical books make plain that he did not take a scholarly approach in the technical, critical sense of that term. Generally he did not lead his students into a consideration of the evidence offered or the views taken by various critics on biblical issues. There are almost no bibliographical references in his discussions. Very occasionally there will be a reference to "the older interpreters," "more recent interpreters," the Talmud (the Jewish body of law and tradition), the Septuagint (a Greek translation of the Old Testament), Luther, and several others, but his primary concern was not to give students an overview of scholarly work in the field.

Nor can it be claimed that Sverdrup made any significant contribution to the advancement of biblical scholarship. There are very few references to the scholars or the critical questions that were coming to the fore during this time, especially in Europe. He did make note of the view that Moses did not write the first five books of the Old Testament but that they were derived from several sources. Sverdrup was not persuaded by that opinion, but it seems fair to say that his main energies were not devoted to such issues.

Sverdrup's treatment of biblical books consisted of a brief discussion of historical setting and authorship, a concise summary of the plan, contents, and leading thoughts of the book, and some reference to the manner in which it fit into the history of Israel and into the Old Testament canon. His stress on such

59

Scriptural features as the decisive moments in Israel's history, God's word of judgment and promise, and the call to man to have faith in God's promises shows his practical concerns. Within that framework his treatment is clear, concise, and careful, enabling the reader to gain a better understanding of the message of God's lordship over history.

A series of unpublished lectures on the character and work of the Holy Spirit sheds additional light on Sverdrup's approach to Scripture and gives evidence of deeper interest in the scholarly issues under debate in Old Testament studies. Speaking of the Spirit's inspirational activities, Sverdrup maintained that the words of the human authors became God's Word because God's Spirit put into their minds the words they should speak and write. He sought to move away from a simple verbal inspiration and did not believe in author ecstasy, or dictation in the ear, nor in obliteration of the uniqueness and individuality of the writers. They were "witnesses" in the truest sense, Sverdrup taught.[3]

Some of these issues were discussed in letters exchanged with his son George. The son, who was doing graduate work at Yale, confronted questions raised by the critical approach to Scripture. Sverdrup saw some value in the newer methodology, but he also suggested that it is possible to get so caught up in details that one misses the central point. The main thing, he stressed, was to understand a biblical book in its entirety and to get hold of the "red thread" that runs through the history of mankind. He maintained that history and revelation are so intertwined in the Old Testament that they cannot be separated. Although Sverdrup did not reject the concerns of the biblical critics, he felt that those concerns were not what mattered most in studying the Scripture.

Perhaps more significant than the details of his handling of individual books of the Bible is the general approach to Scripture reflected in Sverdrup's presentations. It has been suggested that Sverdrup was one of the few Norwegian-American Lutheran

theologians who sought to break out of the constraints of repristination theology by viewing Scripture as a witness to God's
saving activities in history. His point of departure was derived
from some of the newer nineteenth-century approaches that he
had studied in Europe.[4] Sverdrup was not alone, however, in
his ability to challenge the received wisdom.

THE AUGSBURG POSITION

Even before Sverdrup's arrival, Weenaas and Oftedal had
shown their willingness to enter the arena of theological battle,
making Augsburg Seminary a center of opposition to the Norwegian Synod. Strong evidence of this willingness is the remarkable
document called "The Open Declaration" (*Aaben erklæring*),
which the two men published in January, 1874, shortly after
Oftedal came to America.[5] It was a vigorous attack on what was
called Wisconsinism within the Norwegian Synod. That term,
which reflected the strength of the Synod in Wisconsin, was
used by its opponents. Nevertheless, the authors of the declaration stated that they were not criticizing pastors or members of
the Norwegian Synod, but rather an "anti-Christian tendency
. . . supported by a papistic principle, [that] works to dissolve
Christianity in universalism and hierarchy." One effect was a
religious indifference that despised all revivals and signs of
spiritual life in the congregation. The document went on to say
that there was both a theoretical and a practical Catholicism
within Wisconsinism. These were evident in its rationalistic orthodoxy, which restricted theology to dogmatics, dissolving faith
in a dead intellectuality, and in various specific stances associated
with the Synod. The conclusion was that there was no more
possibility of a reconciliation between the Conference and Wisconsinism than between Christ and Belial or fire and water. The
authors indicated their readiness to work to counteract this Wis-
consinist tendency.

Needless to say, this strongly-worded document produced a

vigorous reaction. For years the leaders of the Norwegian Synod felt that it was the most outrageous attack that had been made against them. And many persons outside of the Norwegian Synod, who had also opposed what they regarded as Wisconsinism, felt that the unrestrained language of the declaration was uncalled-for and did not reflect favorably on Oftedal. The repercussions of "The Open Declaration" reverberated for a number of years.

In August of that same year, 1874, Sverdrup and Sven Gunnersen arrived at Augsburg and, together with their friend Oftedal, completed the "new Triumvirate" there. Before long Sverdrup entered vigorously into the religious and theological debates, not hesitating to identify himself with "The Open Declaration." It soon became clear that in Georg Sverdrup the Norwegian Synod had one of its most articulate and forceful opponents.

SVERDRUP'S THEOLOGICAL STANCE

In an article written after he had been in the United States for some time, Sverdrup summarized his differences with the two original Norwegian-American Lutheran church groups. He felt that the theology of the Hauge's Synod, which had grown out of Eielsen's Synod, lacked a correct emphasis on the congregation, but he appreciated this group's insistence on personal Christian experience and commitment. On the other hand, Sverdrup said, the Norwegian Synod stressed the position of the clergy as a teaching office elevated above the congregation's members by learning and insight. In America the strong arm of the secular law could not be used to hold the people together under the clergy, so the Synod sought to use "pure doctrine" as a substitute for secular law, admonishing any member who deviated from it in the smallest particular. Linking himself firmly to the Open Declaration, Sverdrup stated that the zeal for pure doctrine came partly from contacts with German Lutherans of the most extreme confessional and dogmatic tendency, the Missourians. The enthusiastic admiration of the Norwegian Synod for the Missouri Synod led the former to have its pastors educated at St. Louis, where the foremost teacher was "the learned and energetic Professor [C.F.W.] Walther." Training with the Germans, wrote Sverdrup, the Norwegian Synod pastors developed a zeal bordering on fanaticism for the old Lutheran dogmatics and the understanding of Christianity as essentially doctrine. At the same time those Norwegian-American ministers lost much of their connection with their own nationality and the interests that stirred believers in the church of their homeland, Sverdrup believed.[6]

In short, he considered the theological emphases of both these parties to be inadequate. The Conference view—and Sverdrup's—put the congregation in the central position. It is clear, however, that he regarded the Synod as posing the greater threat to the free church that he wanted Norwegian Lutherans to build in America. Doctrine was important but not so important as the new life in Christ. Sverdrup believed that the Synod's Missourianism could only lead to clerical dominance and a lack of true spiritual life.[7]

When Sverdrup and his colleagues spoke of a "Catholicizing tendency" within the Norwegian Synod, they referred to an attitude, an outlook that dissolved the true congregation in order to create a large church from the masses of people, a belief that the Synod was "the orthodox church" and "the one saving church."[8]

Specific theological issues illustrate Sverdrup's differences with the Norwegian Synod. In the 1860s and 1870s the debates centered on absolution, the nature of the Gospel, and the "justification of the world." These arguments can be seen as "the clash of two opposing points of view: the Missourian emphasis on the objectivity of truth and the Haugean and 'orthodox pietistic' emphasis on the personal appropriation of truth." In other words, the difference was between objective and subjective approaches.[9] Seeking to stress the objectivity of truth, the Norwegian Synod maintained that in the Gospel, or word of absolution, the forgiveness of sins is given, presented, and imparted to all who hear it, whether they believe it or not. The forgiveness that God conveys was to them an objective reality, not conditioned by or dependent on the response that man might make to it. This objective emphasis was clearly illustrated in the Synod teaching of the justification of the world, in which the accent was on God's activity: God has with the resurrection of Jesus justified all men without distinction; through His Word and the means of grace He has given this righteousness to all who hear the message. The proclamation of the Word was commanded by God to bring to man the message that from God's side all his sins had been forgiven in Christ. God's justification of all men would not be effective for everyone, however, since some would by their unbelief deny what God had done in Christ. Thus even though all men were justified, according to the Synod view, this reality would be effective only for those who believed the message proclaimed to them.

Georg Sverdrup's opposition to this teaching was clear and sharp. He maintained that since justification by faith was the key article in the Lutheran confessional stance, the differences between the Synod and the Conference on this issue were far from a mere doctrinal dispute; they were also a church strife (*kirkestriden*), a struggle between church bodies concerning how the Lutheran free church was to be built. The basic question, as Sverdrup saw it, was this: which body has been most faithful to the simple Lutheran teaching (*børnelærdom*) as expressed in Luther's *Catechism* and Bishop Erik Pontoppidan's *Explanation* of it?[10]

The term *børnelærdom* was a crucial one in Sverdrup's effort to explain what was wrong with the approach of the Norwegian Synod. The term literally means childhood teaching, but it was used in a somewhat technical way by Sverdrup and others to refer to the simple and basic teachings embodied in the *Catechism* and the *Explanation*. They maintained that *børnelærdom* was far superior to the highly technical and abstruse theological theses and propositional statements that the Norwegian Synod, influenced by the Missouri Synod, subscribed to. This Missourian emphasis, said Sverdrup, "makes no distinction between Christianity and knowledge of pure doctrine, no distinction between God's Word and the pure doctrine, no distinction between the Lutheran church and the church of true believers." Dogmatics replaced God's Word, orthodoxy replaced the new life in God, and the Lutheran church replaced the communion of saints. This Synod tendency led to rationalism and was clearly not what was needed for building the free church in America, Sverdrup asserted.[11]

In his thinking the controversy over justification had developed out of the debate on absolution. The central issue, he maintained, was the forgiveness of sins. He held that the Lutheran church had never distinguished between justification and the forgiveness of sins. According to *børnelærdom*, the two were the same. So the basic issue at stake was this: to *whom* does God give the forgiveness of sins and *when* does He do it? Stated from the human side the question was: *whose* sins are forgiven and *when*? While the Synod taught that from God's side all men were justified and that this took place some 1,800 years ago when Jesus was resurrected from death, Sverdrup felt that this teaching separated justification from faith. It tended to make the forgiveness of sins an automatic, mechanistic occurrence, dependent only on the pastor pronouncing certain words, rather than creating a personal transaction between the merciful God and a poor, lost sinner.

Sverdrup maintained that the contrast between the Synod teaching and *børnelærdom* was clear. To the question: *who* is forgiven by God? the Synod said "all men," while *børnelærdom* said "all penitent and believing sinners." If we ask *when* God forgives sin, the Synod answer was "from the Resurrection, or before,"

while *børnelærdom* said "when we believe." Sverdrup's understanding of justification by faith stressed the importance of a
"personal meeting between the soul and God" and a "personal
relationship between the Father and His children." He argued
that this perspective was lacking in the Missourian teaching on
justification. It was like Catholic teaching in that it blocked the
way for sinners to come to a personal accounting with God. In
his thinking any doctrine that detracted from man's personal
accountability as he stands before God was not faithful to the
Scripture or *børnelærdom*. Sverdrup spoke of a "deep, fundamental difference in the conception of the essence (*kjerne*) of Christianity" as he compared the two perspectives. He maintained
where "justification of the world" was preached, there the
ground was prepared for the clergy to grasp power, as was true
in the state church of Norway.[12]

In another article Sverdrup asserted that "the pure Synod doctrine, which produced fanaticism, should be described as "dead"
rather than "false." More precisely, it could be called "the dogmatic faith." It embraced and held as true certain tenets, certain
interpretations of Holy Scripture, certain theses and forms. It
comforted itself that thus it was right and correct. But this dogmatic faith was not able to bring about conversion and life in
God. The entire cold and rationalistic system lacked "spirit and
life." It also lacked a correct understanding of the work of the
Holy Spirit. It was therefore unavoidable that believers in the
dead doctrine and the dogmatic faith would come into conflict
with those who subscribed to *børnelærdom* and the revival impulses from Norway.[13]

OTHER THEOLOGICAL AND SOCIAL ISSUES

In the 1870s and 1880s a bitter conflict over the doctrine of
predestination arose within the Norwegian Synod. It became
such a divisive issue that in 1887 a segment of that body withdrew, unable to accept the teaching as set forth by some of the

leaders. The controversy "rocked the well-organized Synod to its very foundations."[14]

Since this was a struggle within the Norwegian Synod, the other church bodies generally stayed out of the fray. Sverdrup did write several editorials and articles about the debate, however, which are useful for the light they shed on the development of his attitude toward the Synod and on his own theological stance.

In Sverdrup's thinking there was an inner connection between the Synod teaching of the justification of the world and the teaching of absolute predestination. The two met in the doctrine of conversion, in the question of man's personal responsibility before God. Sverdrup maintained that his own church body, the Conference, accented a personal Christian faith. Such expressions as a *choice* between the world and God, a *decision* wherein man says yes or no, and the *struggle* involved in conversion were thus valid and legitimate. In contrast to that perspective Sverdrup referred to an article by a Norwegian Synod leader in which man was portrayed as being passive when under the influence of the means of grace. This, said Sverdrup, was a stance that those associated with the religious awakenings in Norway could not accept, for it was a denial of the personal element in Christianity. To be sure, salvation was of God alone, but no one could be saved against his will. Grace, by its very nature, was a free gift. As such it could be either received or rejected, kept or lost. In the final analysis man's salvation had two sides: God's willingness to save all and man's willingness to allow himself to be saved. The Missourian teaching, Sverdrup held, did not reflect this duality.[15]

Sverdrup also disagreed with the Norwegian Synod about issues of social ethics, but even those issues grew out of different theological perspectives. One example is the difference in attitude toward the American common school.

During the latter part of the nineteenth century, especially from the 1850s to 1870s, there was a lively discussion among Norwegian immigrants over the merits of that institution. Leading figures in the Norwegian Synod were among those who argued that the common school was inadequate for several reasons, one of which was its exclusion of the teaching of religion. Such people worked to promote a system of parochial schools that would teach the regular school subjects plus religion and Norwegian.[16]

In 1876–1877 Sverdrup stated his views in a two-part article that Theodore Blegen called "the most incisive essay that the common school controversy produced." In it Sverdrup offered a vigorous defense of the American institution. He appealed to Luther's erasure of the false distinction between the sacred ecclesiastical vocations and the worldly callings that, according to Sverdrup, had been widely accepted for centuries prior to Luther's time. Luther held that if one has faith he can please God in any honorable vocation. This outlook opened to the civic sphere the possibility of being God-pleasing, apart from any special consecration or link with the church. Sverdrup thus traced the basic principle that the church and the state can be completely independent of each other to Luther.[17]

Sverdrup maintained that it was in America that Luther's principles concerning the relationship between church and state had been carried through. For "America has dared to establish a secular rule without the blessing of the church, a civic realm whose right to exist is independent of the church." Church and state had their separate functions; one was not to encroach on the province of the other. That meant that the state should not seek to take over the teaching of religion and the church should not usurp the role of teaching those subjects that equip citizens for participation in the common life of society. Sverdrup called the common school "a nursery for good citizens that the state desires, not a nursery for a single denomination or sect." A lack of faith and an emphasis on pure doctrine were involved in the opposition to such schools, according to Sverdrup. Those who believed in the Lutheran principle that church and state could be completely separate ought to encourage parents to send their children to the common school so that they could receive assistance in the task of becoming good citizens.[18]

It is clear from various examples, then, that Sverdrup was opposed to much of what he saw in the purview of the Norwegian Synod. A term that he sometimes used in discussing different perspectives was *aandsretning*. The word might be translated religious or spiritual orientation. Sverdrup once defined it as "the same as a leading thought, a fundamental principle, a life view, which gives a man's work coherence and character, so that a person's course of action can be recognized from one time to the next because it always refers back to the same basic views and always points forward to the same objective."[19] That definition applied to individuals, but Sverdrup also used the term to refer to orientations within church bodies and groups. In contrast to the Missourian *aandsretning*, he said, "we believe that God's Word precedes the pure doctrine and dogmatics. We believe that Christianity in the heart is more important than information about pure doctrine in the head. We believe that the communion of saints is not limited to the Lutheran church but is found outside of and reaches far beyond the Lutheran church." He rejected the type of theology that sought to elevate itself above the congregation and "the dear lay-people" by means of Latin expressions and abstract thought—the type of theology that showed it was clearly not "of the people" by nourishing its vanity with the philosophic abstractions of dogmaticians instead of seeking the simplicity and wisdom of God's Word. Sverdrup's view was that theology exists for the congregation, not vice versa.[20]

CRITICISMS FROM NORWAY

The fact that Georg Sverdrup had established a distinguished academic record as a student in Norway did not exempt him and his colleagues at Augsburg from negative comments by churchmen in that country. Several articles from his early years in America reflect his responses. One such article, written only a few months after his arrival in America, reacted to a statement in a Norwegian journal that had been highly critical of what was called the "endless exaggerations, injustices, and falsehoods" in the Open Declaration issued by Weenas and Oftedal. Sverdrup defended his colleagues and their declaration, noting that he had left Norway to become a theological professor at Augsburg in part because he was attracted by that statement.[21]

A journal called *Kvartal-Skrift* (Quarterly), started by the Augsburg faculty in 1875, also came under fire in Norway. Sverdrup responded with a lengthy article in the very quarterly that had been criticized.[22] Norwegian critics had found three main faults in the Augsburg quarterly: immaturity in thought, lack of clarity in language, and unorthodox teaching. Instead of directly refuting all these criticisms, Sverdrup's response focused on two topics. One had to do with the concept of the church and the other with the relationship between political and religious freedom.

In his response Sverdrup reasserted the view that the unavoidable task of the Conference was to be a symbol of opposition to clerical dominance and rule, both in the state church in Norway and as it expressed itself in the Missourian tendency in America. He related this notion to the church reform struggle that had gone on in Norway since 1814: was the Norwegian church to be a wheel in the state machine, established in such a way that Christianity became a political religion and the pastor a servant of the state? Or should the Norwegian church strive to become an organic being, with each congregation a body gathered about the means of grace, a place where Christianity expressed itself as a power and the pastor became a servant of the congregation? In this struggle two things were crucial: the right of the congregation to choose its pastor and the proper education of pastors to serve in a truly free congregation—a ministerial education that corresponded to new times and new conditions.[23]

One of Sverdrup's controversial stands was his criticism of the tendency of any one church body to look upon itself as *the* church and to consider all other groups as sects or parties. He took up the apparent contradiction between the concept of one body of Christ and the empirical reality of the division of believers into different creeds. Did this division destroy the unity of the body of Christ? Did it mean that only one group was "the church" and the rest were deviant sects? Sverdrup's answer was no. He regarded the divisions in the church as rooted in the fact that each church body had a task or calling given by the Lord. "The work is divided because it is so infinitely great; each one receives his share of the task because he is the one most fitted for this deed." Therefore each church body that had a genuine calling had a right to exist and should not be thought of as outside of "the church." This did not imply indifference or the idea that one church was as good as the next. In Sverdrup's thinking the Lutheran church was the one in which the gospel was most purely preached. But that did not negate the special vocation of other churches which were also part of the body of Christ. Sverdrup then applied this denominational perspective to the Norwegian Lutheran groups in America. He argued that the Conference had a right to exist because God had given it a calling and a command to work. "Is it then the church? No, it is not the church, and neither is the Synod or the Eielsen group the church. They are all servants in the Lord's church on earth." According to Sverdrup, his critics in Norway regarded his views as a slap in the face of Lutheranism because they held that pure doctrine was the visible mark of the church. They believed that the Lutheran church was the only true church because it alone had the pure teaching. Sverdrup quoted at some length from Luther's writings to show that such a view was not supported there.[24]

The other issue — the relationship between political and religious freedom — was raised in Sverdrup's response to criticisms of an article in which his colleage Oftedal had suggested that political liberalism was closely tied to real freedom. The objections astounded Sverdrup, who was also convinced that the two were indeed related.

It is important to note here that both Sverdrup and Oftedal came from families with a liberal political orientation. Further, Sverdrup's response was directed at certain churchmen with conservative outlooks on social issues. Einar Molland has noted that during the 1870s and 1880s there was a crisis in Norway. During that period the religious and intellectual climate changed markedly as positivism and religious skepticism "descended upon Norway like a landslide." A number of those who fought for more political freedom were also identified with this anti-religious stance. Many of the leading churchmen, on the other hand, defended the more conservative viewpoint, both religiously and politically. They wanted to make a sharp distinction between political freedoms and the true inner freedom that came from Christ.[25] Sverdrup was critical of those church leaders—he named F. W. Bugge and J. C. Heuch—who identified Christianity with a political belief that opposed freedom and a more democratic perspective. Reading history enabled one to see a relationship between political and religious freedom, wrote Sverdrup.

He offered a vigorous defense of the American model, a republic with separation of church and state,[26] arguing that such a pattern permitted the church to develop in a manner that was more pleasing to God than was the case in a state church. Such a system did not automatically create Christians. Instead the responsibility for organizing religion was passed to the people. The political freedoms inherent in a republic provided a model from which God's congregations could learn much. Christ and the early Christians did not rely on external authority for building the Christian fellowship, and Christians in America were placed in a similar situation. There was much to be gained, Sverdrup believed, in a setting that forced Christians to rely on their own resources rather than looking to the coercive power of the state.

Sverdrup's roots were in Norway, but he developed a keen appreciation of the values of the American free-church system.

TENSIONS WITHIN THE CONFERENCE

Not only did Sverdrup's vigorous advocacy of his beliefs during his early years in the United States bring him into conflict with the Norwegian Synod and with conservative churchmen in Norway, it also created tension within his own church organization. Not all pastors in the Conference approved of the views and actions of the Augsburg professors—especially Oftedal and Sverdrup. It became apparent in the 1870s and 1880s that there were two main points of view within the Conference. The publication of the Open Declaration in 1874 is often regarded as marking the appearance of the division within the ranks. Some people in the Conference, though they opposed Missourianism, considered the unrestrained language of the declaration unjustified.

Eventually two designations, "the old direction" (*den gamle retning*) and "the new direction" (*den nye retning*), came to be associated with these two perspectives. Those who followed the old direction maintained that they stood for the original Conference outlook—the one that had prevailed in that church body during the first several years of its existence. They said that a new and alien direction had been introduced into the Conference when Oftedal and Sverdrup came to Augsburg and began to make their impact felt within the church. From their point of view Augsburg Seminary had become a source of disturbances and tensions. Sverdrup and Oftedal were the leading spokesmen for the new direction. In various literary organs they championed their views with vigor.

There was a certain amount of vying for influence and control between followers of the two directions. Before attempting to discuss the issues that divided them—and both sides claimed that there were principles at issue, not just personalities—it will be useful to note several instances in which these differences came to the fore.

In 1876, as has been noted, Weenaas resigned as president of Augsburg in order to return to Norway. At its annual meeting that year, the Conference had to decide whether to replace him and with whom. The Augsburg board of directors proposed electing Sverdrup president of the school for one year and calling a theological professor to replace Weenaas. Weenaas proposed calling Pastor B. B. Gjeldaker to be both professor and president. Sverdrup, who was then treasurer of the Conference, counseled against electing a new professor, arguing that it was not wise "from a financial point of view." The Conference was having trouble paying its professors and it would be better to function with the three remaining men than to continue such a financial burden, he said. The action the Conference took was in a sense a compromise: it elected Gjeldaker as the fourth professor of theology and Sverdrup as president of the school.[27]

J. A. Bergh, writing from the perspective of the old direction, noted that the three Augsburg professors (Oftedal, Sverdrup, and Gunnersen) had voted against Gjeldaker. Bergh said that the opposition to Gjeldaker continued and the issue came up again at the next annual meeting. Gjeldaker was advised to accept a call as a pastor, which he soon did. From that time on, said Bergh, "the Conference stood divided in two contending camps." He added that this may have had the appearance of a personal quarrel, but it was really a disagreement about the value of doctrine. It became clear that "Professors Oftedal and Sverdrup represented another churchly view than that held by the founders of the Conference such as Weenaas and Gjeldaker."[28]

Sverdrup had his own interpretation of the incident, using it to demonstrate that the Conference was "filled with church politics." He told about a pastor who tried to persuade him to vote for Gjeldaker by stating that if Gjeldaker were not elected he

74

and his friends would be embittered and form a dissatisfied party detrimental to the work of the church. Sverdrup said at that moment he made up his mind to oppose that manner of doing things.[29]

Whatever the motives involved in the incident, this much is clear: those who came to see themselves as representing the old direction viewed the Gjeldaker matter as an action by new-direction adherents that showed that the latter did not share some of the basic tenets on which the Conference had been founded.

Another incident involved Sverdrup and the president of the Conference, Pastor Johan Olsen. In 1881 Sverdrup published a stinging editorial entitled "As Sheep without a Shepherd."[30] The immediate cause of the statement was the invitation from the presidents of the several Norwegian Lutheran church bodies in America to a "free conference" on church doctrine. The general theme was to be redemption and the forgiveness of sins.

In his editorial Sverdrup stated that the seven theses prepared for the free conference were a "declaration of war" to the spokesmen for *børnelærdom* and congregational freedom. These theses, he said, were nothing more than spiritless Synod doctrine put forth in a little more attractive wording. There was not a word in them about the Holy Spirit. Further, argued Sverdrup, the great longing in the hearts of the people was not simply union of the synods, not peace at any price, not a large and mighty church body, but God's peace and life, the simplicity of the Word, and the freedom of the congregation. He pointed to weaknesses in all of the Norwegian-American synods, including his own. The church officials, he said, practiced church politics instead of taking their stand on the basis of *børnelærdom* and the freedom of the congregation. This could be seen in their support of every pastor, no matter how ungodly his dealings might have been. And so the church bodies and the people had become "as sheep without a shepherd."

Needless to say, President Olsen was not flattered by the editorial. He called it to the attention of the annual meeting of the Conference and said that the church must decide whether it was justified. Sverdrup was given a chance to defend his editorial at that meeting. He offered a lengthy statement in which he sought to provide evidence of the operation of church politics in the Conference. As examples he pointed to the attacks made on the theological professors and, once again, to the refusal to censure erring pastors. Once again he said of the church president: "he does not stand clearly and securely on the basis of *børnelærdom* and the freedom of the congregation." Olsen responded by saying that it was from Augsburg Seminary that politics had come into the church body. He added that it would be difficult to find a bigger work of church politics than Sverdrup's defense.[31]

Pioneer pastor C. L. Clausen, who attended that annual meeting, published a book containing the pertinent statements in this dispute. Clausen clearly opposed Sverdrup's stance, maintaining that the most disgusting of all church politics had been centered at Augsburg since the coming of Oftedal and Sverdrup. He pointed to the Open Declaration as a "manifesto of strife" even within the Conference, speaking of Oftedal as the "father" of that document. He said that Professor Gunnersen did not share that outlook, for Gunnersen was satisfied to be a theological professor. But Sverdrup and Oftedal had greater ambitions: "they were bearers of modern ideas about freedom under the stamp of Christianity, supposedly with a special calling and task to work for them." It was this new element, the modern ideas, that brought tension into the church. Clausen went so far as to say that it was high time for Sverdrup and Oftedal to leave the school unless they made amends.

The annual meeting of the Conference rejected Sverdrup's strong statements about Olsen; it took no responsibility for his editorial; and it asked him to rescind the unkind judgments expressed in his defense. The Conference also disapproved of the statements of Olsen and Clausen and asked them to retract their unkind judgments of Sverdrup. Sverdrup submitted an official apology to Olsen, and the president in turn stated that he had nothing personal against Sverdrup, adding that he respected Sverdrup's "great talents and ability." Clausen, however, protested the actions of the convention. A settlement was reached, but the sharpness of the words that had been uttered was another indication of the differences within the church body.[32]

Some viewed Gunnersen's departure from Augsburg in 1883 as another result of the new and alien element brought into the Conference by Sverdrup and Oftedal. Over the years the two had drawn closer together while Gunnersen had felt more and more removed. When he resigned, Oftedal and Sverdrup felt that they too should submit their resignations. Efforts were made to persuade the men to rescind their actions. Gunnersen was willing to do so, but Oftedal and Sverdrup were not. Finally it was decided to settle the matter by ballot—to re-elect the professors, as it were. Gunnersen did not receive the necessary two-thirds majority vote in his favor, while Sverdrup and Oftedal did. The vote probably reflected the relative strengths of the old and new directions within the Conference. Under the circumstances Gunnersen felt that it was necessary for him to leave his position. Augsburg then had only two theological professors, both leaders of the new direction. Some of those most strongly opposed to Sverdrup and Oftedal argued that three professors—Weenaas, Gjeldaker, and Gunnersen—had been lost because of the political maneuverings of the new-direction leaders.[33]

These examples give evidence of the tensions between the two directions, but what were the principles on which these differences were based? It is not easy to state precisely where they differed because followers of both were orthodox Lutherans in the sense of adhering to the basic Lutheran confessions. The differences between them were not primarily doctrinal or theological.

Yet there were some areas of disagreement. J. A. Bergh published a book in 1884 entitled *Den gamle og nye retning*, in which he sought to distinguish the two. The roots of the old direction were to be found in Norway, Bergh stated. The awakening movements that were important there in the nineteenth century, such as Haugeanism and the Gisle Johnson revival, had stressed the importance of both *life* and *doctrine*. It was this combination, this "orthodox pietism," that through the Conference had been planted on American soil. Bergh said that the old direction had no higher treasure than God's holy Word, no need for the so-called great tasks or special callings. Its adherents were satisfied to work with God's Word for the salvation of souls. Since they had an equal concern for pure doctrine and a pure life, they regarded free conferences for doctrinal discussions and work for church union as legitimate and necessary.[34]

The new direction, said Bergh, was the product of the blending of Gisle Johnson's theology and the Grundtvigian view of life. The latter emphasis put more stress on throwing oneself into life than in getting involved in doctrinal discussions. Specific theological differences between the old and new directions were not great, Bergh asserted, but there was a different perspective on the church. He referred to an essay called "The Church and the Church Bodies," in which Sverdrup had argued that the division of the church into various bodies was justified on the basis of different tasks and callings. Bergh felt that this principle made God responsible for divisions and that it would result in the Reformed tendency to produce one church division after another. It also would lead to a certain indifference to doctrine, for where the accent was on a special task to perform rather than on the pure Word and sacraments, the inclination would be to regard doctrinal differences as relatively unimportant. Bergh felt that the new direction had not entirely escaped these dangers. He noted the scorn of the Augsburg professors for citations from the church fathers, their ill will toward free conferences, and their rejection of theses, propositions, and doctrinal formula-

78

tions. Who, asked Bergh, was going to fight for the truth if it was only life that counted and doctrine was of little or no significance?

Bergh also raised questions about the propriety of theologians publishing a political newspaper,* about Sverdrup's stance on the common school, and about the concept of congregational freedom held by followers of the new direction. Bergh perceived a certain confusion in the idea of the pastoral office and in the tendency to emphasize the authority and power of the church body in a way that restricted congregational freedom. His discussion shows that the major differences between the old and new directions were their attitudes toward doctrinal discussions and their understandings of the church.

Although Sverdrup did not address the issue of the two directions explicitly in his writings, he published several articles about essential principles. In an 1882 series titled "A Free Congregation in a Free Church," he responded to criticism from some old-direction pastors. In addition to elaborating his points about *børnelærdom* and the freedom of the congregation, Sverdrup discussed the relationship of the congregation to the church body. That group exercised its freedom when all its congregations took part in the common endeavor. This meant that they should be genuinely represented at annual meetings so that the decisions of those meetings would truly express the desires of the congregations. Then, said Sverdrup, no congregation would need to say "no" to the decisions that had been made. It was in that framework that the oft-reiterated expression "a free congregation in a free church" was to be understood.[35]

The tensions between the old and new directions within the Conference were most pronounced in the late 1870s and early 1880s. In the years from 1883 to 1890 the strains were muted. Andreas Helland speaks of that period as "years of fruitful progress" in which one did not notice much open tension between

---

*This was a reference to *Folkebladet*, a newspaper discussed in Chapter 5.

the two groups.[36] It seems likely that this surface calm was related to the fact that after Johan Olsen declined re-election as president of the Conference, new-direction men came into the offices of church president, vice-president, and editor of the church newspaper. "Therewith the 'new direction' had all the power, the school, the press, and the leadership in its hands."[37] At any rate, there was a lessening of the strains and sharp language within the Conference during the latter part of the 1880s. During the late 1880s, Sverdrup tried to take advantage of it in a campaign to urge people to support the endowment fund for Augsburg. He felt that uniting in that common cause could serve to bring unity and peace between the two groups.[38] The church union of 1890 brought a realignment of forces and placed the Augsburg men in a different situation. That account, however, belongs to a later chapter.

It is clear that almost from the time of his arrival Georg Sverdrup made his influence as a theologian felt among his fellow Norwegian Lutherans in America. Central to his outlook was an emphasis upon the freedom of the congregation, personal Christianity, and *børnelærdom* as superior to technical theses and propositions. Sverdrup has been called "perhaps the most creative anti-Missourian or anti-repristination theologian among Norwegian Americans."[39] That should not be taken to mean that he constructed a new theological system based on some original organizational principle. Much of what he stressed was traditional. But there was creativity in his attempts to shake off the orthodox scholasticism that many sought to make dominant among Norwegian Lutherans in America. His attempt was given added impetus by his perception of the special calling of his people and of the necessity to grasp the opportunity presented in this democratic setting.

Sometimes the terms *objective* and *subjective* are used to characterize general emphases in Christian thought. It is clear that Sverdrup was closer to the latter—if one understands by it a stress on man's responsibility and accountability in the presence of God, as well as the conscious appropriation of the promises of God which is faith. It was that understanding of Christianity that Sverdrup regarded as essential in the task of building a truly free church among his people in America.

Perhaps the categories used by Leonard Trinterud can be helpful at this point. He spoke of "the evangelical Puritan" and "the rationalistic Puritan" in discussing the roots of certain religious tensions in Colonial America. For the evangelical Puritan "the pilgrimage, the Christian life, was the essential. The theology was important, but it was only the rational explanation of the stages of the pilgrimage. . . . Hence theology was always subservient to preaching and piety in evangelical Puritanism." For the rationalistic Puritan, on the other hand, "theology was primary. Orthodox theology gave a true statement of God's relationship to man, and God would not take lightly any falsification of his glory, wisdom, power, or righteousness. Therefore it was utterly essential that men have and retain right ideas about God and themselves."[40]

It may be that the Lutheran tradition does not fit precisely into the categories as Trinterud has described them. But Lutheranism too has known its own variations of "evangelical" and "rationalistic" emphases. They were present among the Norwegian immigrants. As one who was indebted to the "awakening" impulses in Norway, Sverdrup made clear his choice: the new life in Christ was more important than the niceties of a theological system.

Five

Involved Churchman

Georg Sverdrup was never ordained. That fact enabled him to refer to himself as a layman, even though his was one of the more articulate theological voices among Norwegian Lutherans in America during the latter part of the nineteenth century. An interesting example is his wry comment in a manuscript dealing with the predestination issue in the Norwegian Synod in which he stated that "it is not my intention to get involved in the Election controversy. That is far too high for a layman."[1]

Yet he was involved in a number of areas of church work. He was one of those rare individuals who was capable of both scholarship and leadership. The Conference was small enough so that a person with those qualities would quickly become prominent. In 1874 about 55 Conference pastors and professors served a membership of slightly under 24,000 people. By the time of the merger of 1890 that created the United Church, the Conference secretary could report a roster of over 100 pastors and professors in a membership of more than 70,000.[2] During those years Sverdrup became a leading—and at times controversial—spokesman whose views carried weight both within and without the Conference.

As earlier discussions have indicated, Augsburg Seminary was the main center of his activities. Not only did he spend thirty-three years as a professor at that institution, he also served as secretary of the faculty during his first two years at the school and as its president from 1876 to 1907. Augsburg was the only institution of higher education supported by the Conference and Sverdrup repeatedly stressed the intimate relationship between the school and the church body. He was convinced that the fortunes of the church were indissolubly linked with those of its school.[3]

With Augsburg as his base, Sverdrup was soon involved in other areas of church life and work. The annual reports of the Conference make plain that he was quickly pressed into service. He was elected treasurer of the synod in 1875 and served in that capacity until 1877. A major responsibility of that position was to collect the funds that were sent in to pay the salaries of the professors. He also served as editor or co-editor of the official church paper, *Lutheraneren* (The Lutheran), from 1877–1881 and from 1885–1890. Preaching and speaking trips enabled him to have direct contact with pioneer congregations in various parts of the Midwest. He was elected to several committees, including those having to do with support of Augsburg, publications, free conferences, and church union. His work encompassed many areas in the life of the immigrant church.

Some of his activities need to be seen in the context of the struggle between old direction and new direction in the Conference. The issues at stake in that strife were differing understandings of the church and the value of doctrinal discussions. The record indicates that Sverdrup was not unaware of ways in which power and influence could be used. He was not so prone to church politics as some of his opponents suggested, but he could act firmly and decisively to attain his goals. The mere fact that there might be opposition to his policies did not deter him.

This discussion of Sverdrup as an involved churchman from 1874 to 1890 will focus on his activities in three areas: editing and writing, mission work, and church union. One in which he made notable contributions was editorial and literary work. During those years he had at times an official connection with three newspapers: *Lutheraneren, Kvartal-Skrift,* and *Folkebladet* (The People's Paper). He sought to use these organs to further the causes that he considered important.

Lutheraneren was the official journal of the Conference. Published twice a month, it was intended to be the vehicle by which members would be kept informed and united in the work. At the church's annual meeting in 1877 Sverdrup was named editor of the paper, a position he retained until the middle of 1881. In his opening editorial he set forth his perspective: the paper would continue to bring information about the work of other churches and would give special attention to "our Lutheran countrymen" on both sides of the ocean. It would also continue to lay before the congregations the needs of non-Christian peoples so as to awaken a zeal for mission. He felt that such discussions would enable the Conference to achieve greater understanding of both its position and its calling, which was to follow unswervingly the banner of "our Lutheran confession" as expressed in "our Norwegian *børnelærdom.*"[4]

As editor Sverdrup was in a strategic position to shape and influence the thinking of the young church. His editorials and articles touched on many topics, including the relationships and conditions within the Conference and in other churches, and the importance and needs of Augsburg Seminary. Permeating many of his statements was the conviction that the Conference had a genuine calling from God. Yet it was not a simple task. In many ways the position of the Conference was the most difficult among the Norwegians in this country. As Sverdrup saw it, his church body needed to hold fast to the old *børnelærdom,* to build a seminary uniting Christian earnestness with thorough education, to guard against any tendency for church authority to interfere in the civil sphere, to participate in the great missionary endeavor, to preserve the spiritual link with the Norwegian church without giving up its independence, and to seek its place in a new country. As a young organization the Conference would not always perceive the correct means for realizing those goals, but through strife and struggle it would come to a greater understanding of its role.

Sometimes the strained relationships within the Conference found expression in *Lutheraneren*, as they did in 1879. During the year Sverdrup was involved in exchanges with pioneer pastor C. L. Clausen and Conference president Johan Olsen. The tensions between old and new directions continued to simmer for several years. The new-direction men at Augsburg often spoke out against "clerical rule" (*presteherredømme*) in a free church. Their old-direction opponents sometimes suggested that the real threat in the Conference was "professor dominance" (*professorherredømme*.[5]

Sverdrup's service as sole editor of *Lutheraneren* ended in July, 1881. At the annual meeting of the church that year he was re-elected to the position, but stated that for health reasons he could not accept the election. His replacement, new-direction sympathizer M. F. Gjertsen, was selected and assumed the task that year. In 1885, however, Sverdrup and Oftedal were elected co-editors of the journal. They assumed their positions in October of that year and continued until the middle of 1890. After stating in their opening editorial that they had agreed to assume the post because no other editor was available, the two stressed the necessity of reviving the congregation after its long slumber. They agreed with the statement of the church body that *Lutheraneren* should be "an edifying paper" (*et opbyggelsesblad*).[6]

In 1886 the journal became a weekly. Many of its articles were devotional in nature, designed to edify and to increase mission zeal and interest. A regular feature was a section called "Church News," which contained brief announcements, sometimes with comments, of noteworthy religious items from around the world, with special attention to Norway and the United States. The contents of this section indicate that the tensions within the Conference had for the most part subsided by that time. Augsburg Seminary—its activities and its need for an endowment fund—was a cause that was kept before the people. The editors watched with interest the growing strains and eventual split in the Norwegian Synod over the issue of predestination. Another topic receiving a good deal of comment during the latter part of the 1880s was church union among the Norwegian Lutheran groups in America. Both Sverdrup and Oftedal figured in the deliberations that led to the 1890 union of three Lutheran church groups, and they kept their readers informed of these developments.

Kvartal-Skrift was a quarterly journal whose seven-year existence ran from 1875, the year after Sverdrup's arrival in America, to 1881. The first year it was issued by the Augsburg faculty, after which Sverdrup and Oftedal became its sole editors. Each issue consisted of 48 pages, many of them written by the young Augsburg theologians. Sverdrup, who contributed more than any of the other professors, used the journal as a forum for some of his lengthy theological articles.[7]

The quarterly was advertised as a periodical whose goal was to work for a free congregation in a free church and a free church in a free people.[8] That general goal was spelled out more precisely in several of the editorials with which the journal began each year. The first issue, for example, spoke of the great advantages for church life provided by the freedom of the American setting, as well as some of its dangers. The Augsburg professors announced two main principles that would guide the journal: full self-government of the congregations, involving resistance to clericalism and church factionalism, and the emancipating power of the person of Christ in a personal Christian life, which entailed rejection of an undue emphasis upon pure doctrine (*renlæreri*) and false spirituality. The 1878 editorial emphasized that the

Kvartal-Skrift

for

Den norsk lutherske Kirke

i

Amerika.

Redigeret
af
Prof. Sverdrup og Oftedal.

3die Aargang.

Minneapolis, Minn.
Konferentsens Forlagsforenings Bogtrykkeri.

1877.

Theological journal in which some of Sverdrup's longer essays were published transition to the New World meant that for the first time in its history the Lutheran church was completely independent of secular power and politics. It stood here on its own foundation, with a calling to develop its life in conformity with God's Word. In fact, the Lutheran church was placed in a situation similar to that of the first Christians, for "the first Christian church was a 'free church' just as we are now." In that setting it was important to see both the opportunities and dangers so that the apostolic form of Christianity might be restored.[9] *Kvartal-Skrift* was to be an instrument that would help to achieve those goals.

Folkebladet was a newspaper started by Oftedal in 1877. Its opening issue announced it as a "monthly newspaper for the school and the people." Augsburg was in debt at the time and the publication was designed to help bring the cause to the people. After five issues it ceased because money had been raised to remove the debt. But in 1879 a related cause came along: raising a $50,000 endowment fund (*professorfond*) to ensure the financial viability of the school. *Folkebladet*, with Oftedal as editor, resumed publication as a monthly. In August, 1880, the periodical indicated that in response to requests it would be issued as a weekly, bringing the news to the people from a Christian perspective and in a free churchly spirit.[10]

An examination of the weekly indicates that it contained news and comments on a wide variety of topics, including church matters (both within and without the Conference), developments at Augsburg, political issues, the temperance movement, topics of interest to farmers, wars, news from Scandinavia, America, and around the world. It published novels in serial form and opened its columns to letters from readers, permitting lively and spirited discussion in which burning issues came to the fore. It became one of the leading Scandinavian-language newspapers in the Midwest, advertising itself in 1882 as a publication opposed to machine politics and corruption as well as church politics and party spirit. It favored the participation of Norwegians in civic life, the work for a free congregation, and union in one Norwegian free church. The newspaper sought to resist the unbelief (*vantro*) and free-thought (*fritænkeri*), by which was meant the tendency to form one's beliefs independently of traditional church teachings, that its editors felt were increasing in the 1880s.[11]

In August of 1881 Sverdrup became co-owner and co-editor of the periodical. "The little foundling," as *Folkebladet* was sometimes called, now had both of the new-direction leaders at its helm. This development evoked a good deal of unhappiness in old-direction leaders. A clear statement of their opposition is seen in the 1882 "Declaration of the Thirty," which criticized the new direction and demanded that Sverdrup and Oftedal cease publication of *Folkebladet*, described as that direction's "most pronounced organ." Even Professor Gunnersen was critical of the activities of his colleagues at that point. When he submitted his resignation he stated that "ever since *Folkebladet* came out under a double editorship" the professors at Augsburg had not worked well together. Later he explained that he had come to this country with the understanding that the professors were to give all of their attention to theological work; they were to be exclusively professors and nothing more. *Folkebladet*, he said, was not a spiritual newspaper or one designed for edification, but a political organ.[12]

As noted in the preceding chapter, Gunnersen's resignation led to the resignations of Oftedal and Sverdrup, so that the annual convention of the Conference in 1883 faced a situation in which it had no theological professors. The action at that meeting resulted in the re-election of Sverdrup and Oftedal but not of Gunnerson. Yet the Augsburg board and the Conference convention asked Sverdrup and Oftedal to give up their official connection with a secular journal (*"et verdsligt blad"*) since it was causing so much trouble in the church.[13]

The two professors complied with the request. Even before

the church convention a new editor, J. J. Skørdalsvold, had taken over the job. And the next year the newspaper was transferred to a stock company and was subsequently issued by the Folkebladet Publishing Company. In a farewell statement published in *Folkebladet*, the two men stated that while they could no longer own the periodical, their right to write in *Folkebladet* or other journals "what we believe can be beneficial for church or people" could not be taken from them. They did continue to publish articles in the newspaper; *Folkebladet* was for many more years associated with Augsburg.

The statement by Sverdrup and Oftedal concerning their right to publish is significant also as an expression of their understanding of their role among Norwegian immigrants. They were evidently not convinced that their association with a secular journal had been improper for theologians. They were committed to everything that they felt to be truly *folkelig*, that is, "of the people." The immigrant, Sverdrup once said, finds himself in a setting with a new type of government, a different school system, a new language. He begins to dream of entering into this new society and contributing to its development. Some might say that it is all a temptation that should be avoided. But Sverdrup was convinced that such a view was of little help. He urged the immigrant to become a part of his or her new country by entering fully into its life. His defense of the common school came out of that perspective, as did his belief that the publication of a newspaper that would serve to enlighten "the people" could be a legitimate enterprise for a theologian. This outlook was not unlike that of Grundtvig in its concern for "the people."[14]

Both Sverdrup and Oftedal were aware of the potential of the written word. It enabled them to exert influence. Sverdrup was prolific and his writings are marked by a direct, clear, precise style. His activity as a writer and editor was one of the avenues he traveled to achieve a prominent position among Norwegian immigrants.

FOREIGN MISSION WORK

Foreign mission work was a cause that had Sverdrup's support during his years in America. He wrote and spoke on its behalf, urging the immigrant church to assume a greater role in the endeavor. He regarded the desire to carry the gospel to the "heathen" as one of the fruits of the revivals in Norway. He considered almost all other church work in that country as coerced, but the cause of missions was something that was undertaken freely. Mission work was thus the bond of union among those who voluntarily worked for God's kingdom; it had led to the founding of the Norwegian Mission Society, headquartered at Stavanger, in 1842.[15]

The several Norwegian Lutheran groups in America were initially too small to support foreign mission work on their own. Consequently, interest in the cause was channeled into financial support for the Norwegian Mission Society, but even that enterprise got caught up in the church strife on the American frontier, specifically in the tensions between the Norwegian Synod and the Conference. In 1870 the Norwegian Synod had entered into a relationship with the Norwegian Mission Society whereby the Synod would make financial contributions and have the right to send delegates in an advisory capacity to the general meetings of the Society. Several years later the Conference was granted the same status. The Synod, however, was not pleased with an arrangement in which it was co-operating in Norway with its main opponent in America. It regarded what it termed unionism as contrary to its principles and sought to have the Conference excluded from this form of participation in the Society. Refusing to be drawn into the American squabbles, however, the Society decided that the Conference could continue to be represented in its deliberations.

Sverdrup rejected the charge of unionism and argued that the Norwegian Mission Society was one of the results of the awakening movement that had started with Hans Nielsen Hauge. The

Society, he maintained, stood firmly on the basis of *børnelærdom*, while the Norwegian Synod had been influenced by Missourianism to the extent that it had introduced a conflicting element. He also expressed his firm conviction that the synod or synods that retained a connection with the Norwegian awakening and the Norwegian mission endeavor would be the one or ones that would ultimately constitute the Norwegian Lutheran church in America, while those that severed those links would have a crippled existence. It was a mistake to separate oneself more than necessary from the church in the homeland. Separation in terms of church government and order was necessary, and in time that would also be true of language. But the connections that grew from the deepest roots, including the movement that had produced the mission endeavor, should be maintained. Therefore Sverdrup expressed the hope that his church body—for its own sake, for the sake of the church in Norway, and for the sake of its calling—would increase its support of the Norwegian mission effort.[16]

Sverdrup also viewed joint missionary effort as an instrument of church union in the United States. The church strife in America was due at least in part to the new conditions. There were brothers and sisters in all of the Norwegian Lutheran groups in this country. The day will come, he said, when they will find one another and join in the work for God's kingdom. The joint work in support of foreign missions would hasten that day.

Sverdrup also urged the Norwegian churches in America to undertake mission work on their own. An editorial in *Lutheraneren* in 1880 noted that up to that point the Conference had participated in mission work only by sending money to the Norwegian Mission Society. Yet mission work was of such great importance for the Christian life that the Conference should send out its own missionaries, Sverdrup believed. Augsburg Seminary could provide a man equipped for such work. This could be done while continuing the support of the Society in Norway.[17]

Several years later the mission committee of the Conference proposed the creation of a joint mission society for all of the Norwegian Lutheran churches in America. Sverdrup supported the idea, stressing joint work as a way to overcome church controversy.[18]

In 1885 a mission society was started at Augsburg Seminary. A speech by Sverdrup to the group stressed the dual relationship: students needed missions and missions needed students. He also expressed the hope that Augsburg would be a "hearth" for the "holy fire" of missions.

In 1887 J. P. Hogstad was ordained as a missionary to Madagascar. A special mission festival was held at the Conference annual convention that year, with the sermon delivered by Sverdrup.[19] Two years later Hogstad was followed by Erik H. Tou. Both men were graduates of Augsburg Seminary and were sent out by the Conference under an arrangement with the Norwegian Mission Society. They were the first missionaries with seminary training to go from the Norwegian Lutheran churches in America to a foreign land.

A mission society with the specific purpose of bringing the Christian message to the Jews was the Zion Society for Israel, founded in 1878 with Gunnersen as one of its early leaders. Sverdrup was not directly involved in the society, but the editorials and announcements in *Lutheraneren* indicate that he fully supported its work and objectives.[20]

Sverdrup believed that mission work was of great importance for a free church. A state church, he said, is held together by law, while a free church is held together by the Spirit. Mission work, above all other enterprises, was an indication that God's Spirit was active. The free church would thrive where mission work was carried on energetically.[21]

CHURCH UNION

Church discord was a prominent feature of the Norwegian-American Lutheran scene, but another motif was the desire for unity. Out of that desire came the unions of 1890 and 1917, the two milestones in the reconciliation of Norwegian Lutherans in America. Although the second one is beyond the scope of this study, coming ten years after Sverdrup's death, the developments leading up to the union of 1890 are very much a part of his story. His role in the *foreningssag* (union movement) is a good indication of his stature as a churchman.

The longing for an end to bitterness and conflicts was evident before Sverdrup's arrival in America and continued into the twentieth century. Most of the church bodies desired a reconciliation based on a unity in the faith, but there were differences of opinion about what constituted such unity. The Norwegian Synod, for example, claimed that unity in the faith meant complete doctrinal agreement. That group promoted and encouraged free conferences at which interested individuals met to discuss and debate the controverted theological issues. A number of such gatherings took place in the 1870s and 1880s; their published reports make plain that these pioneer pastors and professors were capable of debating highly technical theological points.[22]

The free conferences, however, possessed no official status; the individuals attending were not empowered to act on behalf of their respective church bodies. These conferences gave way in the mid-1880s to a series of joint meetings. The meetings, which did have official status, also addressed themselves to disputed doctrinal questions, with those present instructed to ascertain whether there was sufficient agreement in doctrine to warrant unity. Through these conferences and meetings leaders came to know each other better and gained a greater understanding of agreements and differences.

A development giving further impetus to the union movement was the withdrawal in 1887 of a group from the Norwegian Synod during the controversy over predestination. That segment, known as the Anti-Missourian Brotherhood, did not want to form still another synod. It invited the Norwegian Augustana Synod, Hauge's Synod, and the Conference to join in negotiations toward union. Hauge's Synod eventually withdrew from the talks, but the remaining three groups joined together in 1890 to form the United Norwegian Lutheran Church in America. Sverdrup was one of the Conference leaders who played an important part in these developments.

Sverdrup's early statements, written before the union movement had gained its full momentum, show that he was not a "pro-union" man. More precisely, they show that he had very definite ideas about what the basis for union should be if it was to be fruitful. In an editorial written in 1878 he spoke of the division among the Norwegian churches as "a tragic necessity." Strife was necessary because unity in the work for spiritual life and congregational freedom was lacking. It was better to have discord, with its zeal and enthusiasm, than a sleeping church. In spite of the injustice and rashness of the struggle, the fundamental motif in the opposition to the clericalism of the Norwegian Synod had been to preserve *børnelærdom* and the link with the awakenings in Norway. There was always the danger of having the form of godliness without its power, the result being "form" Christianity, indifference, and clericalism. The only genuine solution to strife was "our old *børnelærdom* in the free and living congregation."[23]

Sverdrup was convinced that the church controversy had several causes. One was the fact that the state church had not permitted the congregation to be true to its nature, with the result that those who came out of it were immature. He felt that it was easy to be a state church because there was no freedom in it. To be a free church was much more difficult because the demands and responsibilities of freedom accompanied it. Church strife was thus unavoidable because those who had just left the state church could not be expected to agree at once on how to build a free church. Another cause of church discord was the old Norwegian character fault of narrow-mindedness, which expressed itself in petty envy and suspicion. Finally, the importation of Missourianism by the Norwegian Synod had fostered party spirit by its tendency to confuse its teachings with God's Word.

Further, Sverdrup said that God's guidance was to be seen in the struggles. The strife was a chastisement meant for good. On the positive side it indicated that the Spirit had not departed and the salt had not lost its flavor. It indicated a zeal for truth and life. He rejoiced that each of the groups had emphasized certain elements and had been critical of the others. There were beneficial results from such developments for building a free church. These statements should not be taken to mean that Sverdrup was fundamentally opposed to church union. On the contrary, he repeatedly stressed, even in some of his earlier writings, that the goal of "our efforts" was one Norwegian Lutheran free church in America. But that did not mean "peace at any price," union just for the sake of ending the disagreements. The primary goal of a genuinely free church based on Lutheran fundamentals had always to be kept in mind.[24] That meant that certain essential principles must be operative or the end result would be worse than the divisions.

What were those basic principles? One was the conviction that there already existed an inner unity among the Norwegian Lutheran churches in America. It is not necessary to *create* a unity; we *are* one now, he insisted, by virtue of what is held in common. All of the Norwegian bodies were Lutheran and together constituted the Norwegian Lutheran church in America. The common heritage found in all of these congregations included a large measure of unity in church customs and government; the recognition of the Scripture as the source, rule, and guide for faith, doctrine, and life; the acceptance of the generally recognized symbols of the Lutheran church; and the *børnelærdom* which was in a sense a more complete expression of unity than the confessional writings, for it was better known than they were. What more, asked Sverdrup, is needed to form one Lutheran free church when the congregations agree on all of these things?[25]

A corollary of that principle was the conviction that the free conference approach was not the right way to create a united free church. Sverdrup felt that that method did not recognize the fundamental Lutheran unity that already existed. It also tended to foster the detailed and exhaustive doctrinal discussions that he associated with the "theses Christianity" of Missourianism. It sought unity by means of doctrinal consensus. The result was confusion and more division. The era of the free conferences is past, Sverdrup wrote in 1879.

Still, he did not always dismiss the free conference approach as useless. When P. A. Rasmussen, a pastor who played a leading role in the union efforts, issued a statement in 1880 stressing the elements common to the Norwegian Lutherans and calling for a meeting of Norwegian Synod and Conference people to discuss them, Sverdrup responded positively. Rasmussen was at that time a member of the Norwegian Synod, and Sverdrup felt that his statement was an encouraging sign. But when the Minnesota district of the Synod responded to Rasmussen's initiative by stating that even though there were these many elements in common, the Conference still held quite another faith than that confessed in the Scripture and the Lutheran confessions, Sverdrup's enthusiasm cooled. That judgment by the Minnesota district irritated him for a long time. He felt that the Synod had thereby excluded the Conference from the Lutheran church. He repeatedly called upon Synod leaders to retract it. Even at a free conference that he did attend at Holden, Minnesota, in 1883, he stressed the need for a retraction of that pronouncement. In any case, the whole free conference approach was basically at variance with Sverdrup's conviction that a fundamental inner unity was already present among the churches.[26]

A related principle that was significant for Sverdrup was that co-operation among congregations should precede union. Let the congregations work together in such areas as congregational activities, support of foreign missions, and maintaining a joint seminary, said Sverdrup, and this inner unity will find a variety of expressions. Union will then come of its own accord and in its own time.

A final principle has been implied in the above statements: it was the congregations that had to unite. Church union was not something that pastors and professors brought to pass; neither was it the work of lay people alone. The congregations, in their freedom, were the proper instruments of union. When the correct principles for building a truly free church had had time to work themselves out, the congregations would be brought together. Through co-operative efforts they would realize their essential harmony in the Lutheran heritage. One of their options as free congregations would be joining hands in one church body. When that time comes, said Sverdrup, "I will gladly join in such union work."[27]

The momentum of the union movement increased during the latter part of the 1880s, and Sverdrup played a significant part in the proceedings, seeking to direct the course of events in accordance with his principles. The Conference selected him to be on its committee dealing with church union. He attended a joint meeting in 1886 at Gol in Goodhue county, Minnesota, and figured prominently in the discussions. He pointed out that it was high time the groups recognized one another as Lutherans, and he underscored the importance of co-operative efforts. Later, when the Anti-Missourians took the initiative in calling for meetings to discuss union, Sverdrup again represented the Conference as a committee member. To be sure, he had had reservations: as he watched the withdrawals from the Norwegian Synod in the predestination fight, he stated that it was difficult to evaluate the movement—leaders on both sides appeared to be "theses makers," the only question being which one could express himself best and argue most sharply. Yet he felt that underneath the theological sparring, the Anti-Missourians represented a deep longing for a simple Lutheranism and a release from the emptiness of the "theses" approach to Christianity.

Nor did his reservations prevent him from joining the work for union. Indeed, Eugene Fevold has stated that "from 1888 until the union of 1890 no other man was of greater influence in determining the form that the union assumed." He was part of the joint union committee that met in Eau Claire, Wisconsin, in August of 1888. At that meeting three documents were prepared: (1) a settlement (*opgjør*) of the old doctrinal issues; (2) proposed articles of union; and (3) a proposed constitution for the church that was to be formed in 1890. Sverdrup said of the doctrinal settlement that the intention was to bury the old controversies and thereafter seek to stand on the Lutheran confessions. He stressed the establishment of a joint seminary, with an endowment to sustain it, as the most important of the articles of union.[28]

These committee proposals were considered at a joint meeting in Scandinavia, Wisconsin, three months later. That meeting ratified the essentials of the three documents, although Sverdrup's choice of a name for the new church that was to be created ("The Norwegian Lutheran Free Church in America") was changed to "The United Norwegian Lutheran Church in America."[29] During the next year the negotiating churches considered the documents in their respective synods. The Hauge's Synod withdrew, feeling that conditions in the synod were not propitious for merger. That action was a disappointment to Sverdrup and he urged them to be a part of the new church, feeling that they had an important contribution to make. The withdrawal of one did not stop the other bodies, however. In June, 1890, the Conference, the Anti-Missourian Brotherhood, and the Augustana Synod came together to form the United Norwegian Lutheran Church in America. The editors of *Lutheraneren* (Sverdrup and Oftedal) described the events of that day and concluded by saying "so far everything has gone well; praise the Lord."[30] Sverdrup had worked hard in the efforts leading to union. Now his principles for building a genuinely free Lutheran church in America were to find expression in a new church body. Subsequent events showed that some of them encountered more difficulties than he had anticipated.

"The story of America," says one student of religion in America, "is the story of uprooted emigrant and immigrant people, ever moving rapidly onward through space so vast that space came to take precedence over time in the formation of their most cherished ideals."[31] The task of the churches was to try to meet the spiritual needs of these large numbers of people on the move. In the process American Christianity came to be marked by a type of activism: involvement in the practical tasks of ministering to the millions of people coming to these shores. The luxury of developing impressive theological systems had to yield to the more immediate tasks of building churches, schools, and other institutions in this new environment.

Georg Sverdrup's activities during his early years in America can be seen in that context. The main goal, as he saw it, was to assist his fellow Norwegian Americans in making the right transition from a state church to a free church. It was important for those involved in laying the foundations to do their job correctly. He committed himself to that task and sought to impart his vision to others. He used a variety of means to accomplish what he felt to be worthy objectives.

J. A. Bergh once characterized Sverdrup as a "born leader." He went on to say that Sverdrup would set a goal and with "masterful ability" work for its attainment. "What wouldn't bend had to break. He thereby created friends, admirers, and opponents."[32] Those qualities and results were clearly present during the years he was involved in the church work of the Conference. What he might have accomplished as a scholar in another setting is open to conjecture. His significant contributions to building the church among immigrant pioneers are clear. Even those who disagreed with what he sought to do in his early years in America recognized the clarity of his vision and his dedication to objectives.

That persistence continued as he sought his role in the newly formed church, even when it brought difficulties greater than he had ever before experienced.

PART THREE
AMERICAN EDUCATOR, THEOLOGIAN, CHURCHMAN:
BUILDING NEW STRUCTURES (1890–1907)

Six

Defending A Concept of Theological Education

Henry Steele Commager spoke of the decade of the 1890s as "the watershed of American history." He contended that on one side of that period was an America that was predominantly agricultural, conforming intellectually to the political, economic, and moral principles inherited from the seventeenth and eighteenth centuries. On the other side was the modern America, predominantly urban and industrial, involved in and troubled by the problems and perplexities of a new age. The nineties, he said, marked the end of one era and the beginning of another.[1]

Commager's thesis applies to the broad spectrum of American society. Speaking more specifically of religious developments, A. M. Schlesinger, Sr., noted two great challenges to organized religion in America during the last quarter of the nineteenth century, "the one to its system of thought, the other to its social program."[2] In a number of the main line American denominations certain fundamental theological and ethical issues came to the fore with great intensity. Out of that ferment came such varied products as heresy trials, the social gospel movement, and the Fundamentalist-Modernist controversy.

One may question the extent to which Norwegian Lutheran immigrants were directly influenced by those developments.

Their seminaries and religious leaders remained largely untouched by the "modern" theologies, and their linguistic and cultural patterns shielded them from many of these impulses. It cannot be claimed that they were completely isolated from the world around them, for lectures and publications made them aware of new ways of thinking. But to a large extent they were preoccupied with the problems of adjusting to the patterns of life in the New World.

In that context the decade of the nineties was also a significant period for Norwegian Lutheran immigrants. As noted earlier, three separate church bodies joined together in 1890 to form the United Norwegian Lutheran Church in America. That event caused much joy, for it seemed to herald a new direction. Some of the descriptions of the union day reflect the intensity of feeling as separated brethren found one another and joined hands in a common endeavor.[3]

The decade of the 1890s was important also in the history of Augsburg Seminary and in the life of Georg Sverdrup. During that period, Augsburg became the focus of a bitter controversy in which Sverdrup was clearly involved. The struggle altered the course of both the school and the man.

In 1890 it appeared that Augsburg Seminary had a promising future ahead of it. The United Church had become the largest Norwegian Lutheran group in America. The articles of union accepted by the three uniting bodies stated that Augsburg was to be the seminary of the new church. The school thus would have a broader base of support and would serve a larger constituency. Its staff of theological professors was to be increased from two to five. Named to join the Conference men Sverdrup and Oftedal were F. A. Schmidt and M. O. Bøckman from the Anti-Missourians and D. Lysnes of the Norwegian Augustana Synod. Professor Lysnes died before assuming the position, and in 1891 Emil G. Lund was named as the fifth professor. The enrollment in the theological department increased as the seminaries of the other two groups consolidated with Augsburg. The Minneapolis school, with Sverdrup as president, seemed destined to become an important center for the religious life of Norwegian immigrants.

Augsburg Seminary did not become that focal institution. Several years after the 1890 union, continued controversy prompted the majority within the United Church to establish a new theological school. The theological department at Augsburg continued to exist until well into the twentieth century, but it served a much smaller group. Its defenders could claim that the ordeal had enabled the school to achieve greater clarity of principle and purpose, but it cannot be denied that there was also a greatly reduced sphere of influence in which those principles could be put to work.[4]

To understand the nature of the controversy that developed in the 1890s, it is necessary to look again at the main features of Augsburg's pattern of education. The aspects of the 1874 plan that had been put into practice resulted in a school with three levels: a common class (*fællesklasse*) for all entering students, a four-year college-level Greek department (*græskskole*), and a three-year theological department. These levels were considered organically related to one another, so that the institution was regarded as one school with several departments. Sverdrup and Oftedal had championed the principles embodied in that pattern, and as the Conference entered the 1890 union they stressed that years of experience had shown it to be the best one for developing Lutheran pastors to serve the American congregations.[5] They were convinced that Augsburg should be preserved as it was at the time of the union. The articles of union had given some assurances to that effect in the statement, "the preparatory departments at Augsburg Seminary . . . shall be conducted in the same way as formerly for at least one year after the union is effected." That rather general pronouncement, which applied to the common class and the Greek department, seemed to represent a commitment on the part of the new church body to the idea that no immediate changes would be made. At the same time, the statement implied that the new church was not committing itself to the Augsburg system over the long term.[6]

What precipitated the struggle over the "school issue" in the newly formed church? Two related factors were important. One was the existence within the church of another concept of theological education. That difference manifested itself as early as the first annual meeting of the United Church in 1890, where Pastor J. M. Dahl said that the church needed a college as well as a seminary. He also felt that the two should be separated from each other, though not by so great a distance that they would become strangers to one another. Professor F. A. Schmidt, who was to be Sverdrup's colleague at Augsburg, expressed similar opinions. He stated that the preparatory school should be separated from Augsburg Seminary so that the two would be independent. People have always returned to the view, he said, that it is not a fortunate arrangement to have the two institutions together.[7] Here was a call for a clear distinction between a seminary (*præsteskole*) and a college that could be used to prepare students for the study of theology.

The second factor was related. Augsburg Seminary was not the only institution of higher learning that was to be part of the United Church. The new synod, at its initial meeting, adopted a resolution stating that "St. Olaf College in Northfield, Minnesota, is to be the college of the United Norwegian Lutheran Church." It also stated that the church body pledged its support of St. Olaf. Many regarded the school as a worthy gift that should not be refused; its capable staff was seen as a resource that would make a valuable contribution to the church.[8]

St. Olaf's School (later St. Olaf College) was started in 1874 and operated for a number of years as an academy. Beginning in the late 1880s its program was gradually upgraded to the college level. The school was owned and operated as a private corporation, although its early leaders were men associated with the Anti-Missourian Brotherhood during that group's brief existence. The Brotherhood had regarded St. Olaf as its educational institution.

Leaders of Augsburg Seminary came to regard this move to adopt St. Olaf as the college of the church as a threat to Augsburg's preparatory departments and to its concept of theological education. The result was contention and misunderstandings over what was called the school question. The debates created the impression of a St. Olaf faction pitted against the supporters of Augsburg.

As early as 1891 the mistrust and suspicions found expression in the pages of some Scandinavian-language newspapers. In January of that year *Skandinaven* published a piece by a person who signed himself "A. Eriksen." The article consisted of a couple of letters that were supposedly sent to "Mr. Eriksen" by an Augsburg student, letters in which negative comments were made about the quality of the program at Augsburg. Academic demands were said to have sunk to a minimum. Students reportedly studied whatever they wanted, neglecting Greek and Latin if they were not interested in those subjects. The school, with its several levels, was said to be neither fish nor fowl. Later that year it was learned that the person who signed himself "A. Eriksen" was in reality Albert E. Egge, a teacher at St. Olaf.[9]

Folkebladet, which reflected Augsburg's interests, was quick to pick up the matter. In 1891 many of its issues carried articles and exchanges dealing with some facet of the debate. F. A. Schmidt, who by that time was teaching at Augsburg, focused on the Augsburg educational plan. A former Anti-Missourian leader, he maintained that when the three bodies united in 1890 they had formed a new church. That meant that none of the uniting parties could demand that its institutions remain unaltered in the new body. He further argued that the seminary (*præsteskole*) referred to in the articles of union was clearly only

*First portion of Old Main at Augsburg, constructed
in the early 1870s; two wings were added later*
(From A. Helland's *Augsburg Seminar gjennem femti aar;* used by permission)

Augsburg's theological department, with its professors and students. The preparatory departments were not "inextricably united" with the church's seminary, he claimed, and the question of whether the two should be united was a legitimate topic for discussion. Schmidt's own opinion was that in the long run the church would be best served when it had colleges that were separated from the theological seminary. The church, he stated, needed independent-minded clergy; the type of education in which young men were under the same teachers and authorities from beginning to end led to uniformity, immaturity, and one-sidedness.[10]

That article led to a number of editorials, defenses, and responses. Schmidt's stance was clearly at variance with Sverdrup's position. The latter stated in his 1891 report to the church that

New Main building at Augsburg, dedicated in 1902
(From A. Helland's *Augsburg Seminar gjennem femti aar;* used by permission)

the connection between the preparatory departments and the seminary should be kept as close as possible. He maintained that the instruction in the preparatory departments provided the best basis for a fruitful study of theology. He also felt that the theological professors and students had a beneficial influence on the younger men.[11]

Other statements in *Folkebladet* reflected the complaint of the Augsburg people that St. Olaf had been brought into the church in an unwise and unfair manner. That school, it was noted, was not even mentioned in the articles of union. Instead, it was brought up at the uniting convention and, in the euphoria of the moment, was accepted as the college of the church without proper consideration given to what was being done.[12] Some of the Augsburg supporters even came to feel that there was a conspiracy on the part of some Anti-Missourians, Augustanans, and old-direction Conference people. As the Augsburg people saw it, these groups opposed Augsburg's unique principles of theological education; their goal was to destroy that system by eliminating Augsburg's preparatory departments and promoting St. Olaf as the college of the church.

This conspiracy, as Carl Chrislock has written, "existed more in the minds of its proponents than in the real world." The evidence does not support the existence of a "monolithic majority" bent on eliminating Augsburg's educational pattern. A reading of the annual reports of the United Church indicates that most of the leaders were earnestly searching for a compromise that would preserve unity. Augsburg supporters argued for a retention of the Augsburg model; St. Olaf supporters sought to promote its cause; still others hoped to find a solution that would enable the church to settle this matter and get on with its tasks.[13]

The controversy over Augsburg also had legal implications, which surfaced in what came to be known as the transfer issue. The articles of union had stated that the new church body was to be incorporated as soon as possible and that all school property the three bodies possessed at the time of the union was to be transferred to the new church. The boards of trustees of the earlier churches were to continue to function only until the new church was incorporated.[14]

Augsburg had served as the school of the Conference, but the Conference had not been legally incorporated. It was not in a position to make a legal transfer of the school. Augsburg was instead controlled by its own board of trustees, with Oftedal as chairman. When the United Church was incorporated in 1891, it was expected that the Augsburg board would transfer the school so that the church body could gain control of its seminary. That was not done, however. The Augsburg-St. Olaf discussions had alerted Augsburg supporters to the possibility of changes in its program once control passed from their hands. And there were legal complications: Judge Andreas Ueland, whose legal services had been engaged by the United Church, said in 1891 that in his opinion it would be a betrayal of trust if the Augsburg and St. Olaf boards were to transfer their property to the new body. Such transfers might be made, but they could be challenged and would likely be hindered or set aside. As he stated it, "while the transfers would thus be voidable they would not be void. Until attacked and set aside by the Court they would be operative and vest title in the new corporation."[15]

The Augsburg board regarded this as additional justification for its refusal to make the transfer. Yet the United Church persisted in its contention that fulfillment of the articles of union meant that it had a right to gain control of the seminary. A solution seemed possible in the spring of 1892, when two Minnesota attorneys, William S. Pattee and Seldon Bacon, put forth a proposal. This Pattee-Bacon plan agreed that the direct transfer of the schools by the boards of trustees would be a questionable action. Their suggested resolution to the impasse was to "make the members of (delegates to) the Annual Meeting of the United Church the members of the several corporations (Augsburg and St. Olaf) . . . and the sole members thereof, respectively. This will vest all the control of the Institutions in the United Church; second it will keep the legal title of the property where in law it is very important that it should be kept, viz. in the corporations named." In other words, there would be three corporations: the United Church, Augsburg Seminary, and St. Olaf College. The delegates to the United Church would also constitute the sole members of the other two. Legally the corporations would be separate and distinct; from a practical point of view the membership would be identical.

The Pattee-Bacon plan was regarded by many as a good solution to the problem, but the Augsburg board did not go along with the proposal. The annual meeting of the church in 1892, held in Dawson, Minnesota, was dominated by the school issue. The meeting went on record as suggesting that the Augsburg board transfer ownership to the church body in accordance with the proposed plan. Church president Gjermund Hoyme too noted in his report that the transfer of Augsburg Seminary had not taken place. He expressed his feeling that the church had a "contractual and moral right" to own the school. In his opinion the school's preparatory departments—considered as "a pro-seminar"—were both necessary and desirable. On the assumption that both schools would be transferred to the church, the church's college committee recommended the same thing: retain the preparatory departments as a proseminar, with one president over the entire school. It also urged St. Olaf teachers to remind students that saving souls for God's kingdom is the noblest work of all and to encourage qualified students to study theology when they finished college.[16]

But the debates and discussions at the Dawson meeting continued, with Oftedal and Sverdrup taking a prominent part in them. Sverdrup urged proceeding slowly, saying that there was a sense in which the original articles of union could not be fulfilled legally. He maintained that it would be necessary to work for a new agreement. He also stated that St. Olaf was the reason for "so much bad blood among us."

Finally, Pastor J. N. Kildahl proposed a congregational referendum to decide whether the United Church should maintain both St. Olaf and the college department at Augsburg, or, if not both, which one. The congregations were to report by December 31, 1892. The school or schools chosen would be transferred, debt free, before the next annual meeting so that the church could get full control. And the church body was to have the right to "establish, regulate, and operate" the school or schools chosen in the manner decided upon by its annual meeting. That proposal was approved by the annual convention, reflecting the desire of many to get the matter settled once and for all.

The school issue was still unresolved, however, by the time of the next annual meeting of the synod in Minneapolis. The congregational referendum had favored Augsburg, but many congregations had voted for the school on the condition that a transfer would be made. The vote could be interpreted in favor of St. Olaf if the Augsburg board continued its refusal to make the transfer. The Augsburg board had received a legal opinion indicating that the best interests of the school might not be served by the Pattee-Bacon plan. A large and changing constituency, such as that of the church's annual conventions, would be less apt to look after the school's specific concerns than would a smaller governing body. The Augsburg board refused to make the transfer.[17]

The school question had troubled the new church for several years. There was a clear mandate to get the issue settled. President Hoyme made a proposal to the 1893 convention that seemed to go far toward meeting the demands of the Augsburg people. He proposed that the United Church would operate and support only one college—Augsburg. The 1890 action making St. Olaf the college of the church would be rescinded. The United Church would promise to support the college department at Augsburg, provided its board would transfer "full and unrestricted" control of the school before the close of the annual meeting, or by June 30, 1893, at the latest. The convention adopted the basic provisions of this proposal, even though it meant that St. Olaf was cut adrift. The deadline was changed to July 15, 1893, but this stipulation was added: if the Augsburg board did not make the transfer, the board of trustees of the United Church was empowered to move its seminary to another location and operate it there until the next convention. The assumption was that the Augsburg people would accept, since so much had been conceded to them. If they did not, however, the church was prepared to move in another direction.[18]

The Augsburg board did not accept the proposal. By this time Augsburg supporters had come to feel that the majority in the United Church was determined to get control of Augsburg and change its character. They noted that at the annual meeting their own proposals for resolving the impasse had been defeated, while those of the majority were accepted. They felt that they had an obligation to retain control of the school until they received guarantees that its essential nature, as it had been developed by the former Conference, would be maintained. From their perspective Hoyme's proposal to support Augsburg while abandoning St. Olaf could be interpreted as an attempt to find some means to gain control of Augsburg so as to change its preparatory departments into a humanistic college similar in nature to St. Olaf.[19]

Both Oftedal and Sverdrup then submitted their resignations as professors of the United Church on June 14, 1893, with Sverdrup pointing to a basic disagreement over principles of theological education and church work as the fundamental cause. There had been times in earlier years when both men had resigned from their posts; then they had been asked to reconsider so that the church might continue to have the benefit of their service. Now their resignations were accepted, and Prof. M. O. Bøckman was named to replace Sverdrup as president of the church's seminary.

It should be noted that the two men had resigned as United Church professors, not as Augsburg professors. The school had not been transferred to the church body. Supporters called "Friends of Augsburg" rallied to the cause, urging Sverdrup and Oftedal to remain at the school. The two men agreed to do so.[20] The United Church, meanwhile, moved to establish a seminary at another Minneapolis location. Three of the Augsburg professors and a number of the students moved to the new site. Augsburg supporters regarded that action as a violation of the articles of union, since that document had stipulated that Augsburg was to be the seminary of the church. The Friends of Augsburg initially thought of themselves as a minority within the United Church, working for the realization of Augsburg's principles. In reality they had broken with the synod. That fact was

116

recognized when the group organized as the Lutheran Free Church (Den lutherske frikirke) in 1897. Augsburg was associated with that body until both church and college became part of the American Lutheran Church in 1963.

The 1893 breach was not the end of the legal maneuverings in connection with Augsburg. Litigation was undertaken as both sides struggled for control of the property. Finally, near the end of the 1890s, a settlement was reached. Legal control of the property remained in the hands of those who had supported the school, while endowment funds and a portion of the Augsburg library went to the United Church. Thus ended a very bitter episode in the history of Norwegian Lutherans in America.[21]

Georg Sverdrup was not in the forefront of the legal battles and proceedings centering on Augsburg to the same degree as Sven Oftedal, chairman of the board of trustees. But Sverdrup was clearly the leader in setting the tone and in articulating the underlying educational philosophy involved. In establishing his position, Sverdrup published a series of important articles in *Folkebladet* during the 1890s.[22] In them he promoted what he called *menighedsmæssig presteuddannelse*—a ministerial education in conformity with the origin, nature, and goals of the free and living congregation in America. Such an education would produce a pastor who truly understood the free church and who would work for its well-being. He argued that such an education would remove the old divisions of class and caste that tended to separate the pastor from the members of the congregation.

Sverdrup contrasted the type of theological education that he advocated with what he called humanism, defined as a special kind of education that used the ancient Greek and Latin classics as the proper means of instruction. The study of these and other languages was not necessarily humanistic if undertaken for its practical benefits, but humanism in its pure and finished form, Sverdrup contended, had as its starting point the idea that what is truly human is something quite different from that which is

117

Christian. The truly human is found in its purity only where Christianity has not had any influence—among the pagan people who lived, thought, and wrote before Christianity came into the world. "Thus the true humanists regard Christianity as a disturbance of the human in its truth and beauty, a disturbance of the noble Greek culture. And so everyone who desires to become educated must return to this beautiful culture in order to find man in his perfection and must shape himself thereafter." Humanism operated under the assumption that man is good by nature. To become truly educated this nature only needs to put on the Greek and Roman forms. "Then the natural has become the human and there is a union of the good and the beautiful."[23]

Sverdrup maintained that in the state church system in Norway, the clergy and other members of the official class received a humanistic training in the Latin schools. The students were encouraged to absorb classical culture as the means by which they might become truly educated. The result of such training, he argued, was that the clergy were removed from the people in the congregations. Class differences prevented or destroyed the interaction that was so vital to Sverdrup and his Augsburg colleagues.

Sverdrup also held that one who consistently followed the principles of humanism tended to maintain his distance from Christianity, even when he studied theology. That person studied theology as another might study jurisprudence or medicine—as an object outside of himself, or as a historical or philosophical phenomenon. If such a person became a pastor, he preached what he had learned, not what he had experienced. He dealt with religion as something that was good enough for the simple man but had little significance for those who were educated. Sometimes it is maintained, Sverdrup said, that the humanistic pattern is the best preparation for the study of theology. Sverdrup came to the opposite conclusion. He stressed that humanism led to aristocracy of spirit and to rationalism. It was

118

only by a fortunate inconsistency that a good humanist sometimes becomes a good theologian. A preparation for the study of theology is needed, he asserted, but it ought to be shaped in accordance with the demands of theology. An education in the humanistic spirit, such as he believed St. Olaf offered, was not "the one thing needful," for it was destructive of spiritual life and created feelings of superiority.

Sverdrup's stance was related to his view that the age in which he lived was "the era of the congregation." For hundreds of years, he held, this unit had been "buried" and suppressed either by the papacy or the state church. But now a new opportunity had presented itself: the chance to rebuild the congregation in its correct apostolic form. Theological education must seek to further that goal. It should not lead the student away from the congregation and its work, but should instead foster a living relationship between the two. The course of the theological students was to be "from the congregation, through the seminary and back to the congregation." Augsburg's preparatory departments would encourage that pattern; a humanistic college would tend to project the divisive tendencies of the old state church onto the American scene.[24]

Sverdrup also stressed that in the seminary the main studies should be Scripture and history—"God's revelation and mankind's self-revelation." The one who was to be a pastor needed to have spiritual insight into the way of salvation for himself and for all mankind. And he who wished to enter confidently into the conflicts of his age needed a thorough grasp of church history so as to avoid being led astray as the church had been so often in the past. This Scriptural-historical focus, it will be noted, deemphasizes the role of a theological system. Sverdrup explicitly stated that the struggle over Augsburg was the result of the conflict between the state-churchly and the free-churchly views of the congregation and the pastor's position in it. He maintained that the strife within the United Church was beneficial in the

119

sense that it produced a clarification of the issues. He felt that Augsburg Seminary thereafter functioned with a greater inner harmony and that the discussions had made its unique principles of theological education more widely known. "The Seminary has prospered more than ever," stated the Augsburg catalog for 1896–1897.[25]

The tendency to view the conflict of the 1890s in terms of humanism on the one hand and the Augsburg educational philosophy on the other led to a degree of anti-intellectual emphasis and the closer identification of the school with the "awakening" impulses that had come from Norway. A catalog from the mid-1890s described the theological department as offering "a thorough and scientific course in theology," but it added that "the end . . . is to develop the spiritual side of the student and make him an earnest, consecrated, and well-trained worker in the vineyard of our Lord." A statement appearing in the 1899–1900 catalog and repeated for a number of years thereafter underscored that emphasis: "Spiritual life and Christian character are considered of infinitely higher importance than mere knowledge. No amount of reading, no memorizing of facts, no mental or intellectual ability are of any real value to the Christian minister without personal experience of saving grace and firm and manly conviction of the truth as it is in Jesus."[26] Augsburg was to guard against those who regarded theological education as being essentially human erudition and book learning (bogstavlærdommen), as well as against the false spirituality that claimed that no time and work were necessary by way of preparation. Without the Spirit, Augsburg professors believed, the letter remained dead and the prophetic word would remain silent. The awakening impulses in Norway that had begun with Hans Nielsen Hauge were seen as now transplanted to this free land where all differences of class and caste were eliminated. Here there was the possibility of a new beginning for God's congregation, and Augsburg's calling and task were to work for its realization. Such work would have an impact in both America and Norway.[27]

Katalog

for

Augsburg Seminarium,

Minneapolis, Minn.

21de Skole-Aar

1890-91.

Minneapolis, Minn.
Augsburg Publishing House's Trykkeri,
1891.

Title page of Catalog listing requirements and course offerings at Augsburg in 1890–91 (Courtesy Augsburg College Archives)

It should be noted once again that whatever anti-intellectual tendencies did exist at Augsburg were certainly not the result of any intellectual deficiencies on Sverdrup's part. He had a distinguished academic background and in his day was one of the better educated men among Norwegians in America. He was, as Carl Chrislock has written, "an acknowledged member of the Norwegian-American community's intellectual elite who chose to champion an anti-elitist position."[28]

Thus it was within the framework of a divinity school committed to the principles propounded by Sverdrup and championed by Oftedal—and serving primarily the Lutheran Free Church—that Augsburg Seminary entered the twentieth century. Its program included a commitment to a single institution with several levels or departments. Such was its status at the time of Sverdrup's death in 1907.

It has been many years since the Augsburg Plan was formulated and later vigorously defended in the Augsburg-St. Olaf controversy of the 1890s. Yet it is important to try to understand Sverdrup's stance. Why did he take this anti-elitist position? Why did he reject so vigorously what he felt to be humanism? On the surface his views on theological education might seem hard to reconcile with his attitude toward the American common school. That institution, it will be remembered, received Sverdrup's vigorous support, even though it did not offer religious instruction. He appealed to Luther's principles on the separation of church and state and urged the immigrants to send their children to this bastion of democracy. In those writings, he stressed that neither Christianity in general nor the Lutheran church in particular were fragile institutions. Christians, he said, should seek to be the salt of the earth, but that would only happen as they participated openly in the life of the free people.

Although there may indeed be some inconsistencies in Sverdrup's thinking at this point, explanations can be found. Certainly part of the reason is his emphasis on "the people." He considered a thing to be helpful, valuable, and beneficial if it was *folkelig*, that is, if it showed a genuine feeling for the people. The common school could be defended because it was profoundly *folkelig*. It served to uplift the people, enabling them to become useful and worthy citizens of their democracy. The humanistic school, as Sverdrup defined it, was just the opposite. He called it *ufolkelig* because it tended to create a caste of persons who considered themselves superior and so led to divisions in society. In short, Sverdrup felt that there was something very undemocratic in humanism. As a school catalog stated: "It is also an essential principle of Augsburg Seminary, that no so-called higher education, which tends to develop aristocratical or hierarchical tendencies among the students, is Christian in character or in accordance with the highest interests of a free people and its institutions."[29]

Another important element of Sverdrup's position was his desire to restore what he felt was the biblical congregation. This was the time to break out of the old ways to try to create something new. Theological education too must become genuinely *menighedsmæssig*—truly in harmony with the free and living congregation.[30]

A third factor that deserves to be noted is the impact of the currents of new thought that emerged near the end of the nineteenth century. Reference was made in an earlier chapter to Einar Molland's statement about religious skepticism and positivism descending upon Norway "like a landslide" in the 1870s and 1880s. The threat of unbelief (*vantro*) and free-thought (*fritænkeri*) in the leading Norwegian intellectual circles seemed real. Sverdrup was aware of developments in Norway. He read newspapers and journals from that country and in 1886 returned for a visit. His impressions were published in a series of articles in *Folkebladet* and *Lutheraneren*.[31] He expressed disappointment that a writer such as Bjørnstjerne Bjørnson had openly espoused *fritænkeri*. He was also dismayed that some of the conservative pastors who wanted to preserve the old order had joined hands

with the freethinkers by resisting the proposals of his brother
Jakob Sverdrup, head of the department of ecclesiastical affairs
in the Norwegian Cabinet, for a greater measure of congregational freedom. The resolution of this struggle, said Georg Sverdrup, could happen "only in a free church."[32]

The situation in America was different, to be sure, for here
there was no state church. But the new ideas were being felt in
the New World too. Visiting lecturers made the immigrants aware
of these impulses. As Sverdrup viewed the situation in America,
especially among Norwegian immigrants, he saw two basic
threats. On one side were those pastors, still imbued with the
state church mentality, who sought to preserve Christianity by
keeping it in the hands of the clergy. On the other side were
unbelief and free thought, with their denials of the essential
message of Christianity, an outlook that led to rationalism. Both
threats, Sverdrup believed, had to be resisted. Successful resistance necessitated the restoration of the free and living congregation. Theological education would become what it should be only
when it served that great objective.

A helpful summary of Sverdrup's attitude toward these new
ideas can be found in a 1903 letter to Norwegian bishop J. C.
Heuch.[33] Heuch had published a book titled *Mod strømmen*
(*Against the Current*), a work characterized by Molland as "a document unparalleled in religious fervor, eloquent pathos, and de-
magogic appeal."[34] It was a sharp attack on the "modern" theologians who were, said Heuch, preaching a new message. He
contended that a remarkable phenomenon had appeared on the
Norwegian scene: rationalism was being proclaimed by Christian
men. The message of these theologians, so inclined toward modern criticism and scientific research, was in reality a denial of
certain essential elements in Christianity.[35]

When Sverdrup wrote to thank Heuch for the copy of the book
he had received, he commended the bishop for his reply to the
rationalistic tendency present in the theological faculty. Sverdrup

then went on to wish that Heuch had noted the connection between a state church system and modern rationalism in Norway. Where the church was a function of the state, led by politicians and political considerations, it was to be expected that such a message could result, he asserted. So long as the church permitted the state to educate and select its pastors, this danger would be present. He concluded the letter: "Let the state have as many theological faculties as it wishes, but let the church have a 'pastor's school' (*presteskole*). Then the theological teachers will become responsible servants of the church instead of the present irresponsible scholars for whom German scholarship is the rule and guide."

Nevertheless, it would be incorrect to characterize Sverdrup's outlook as anti–intellectual fundamentalism. His stance against humanism might better be seen as a variation of a perspective that has appeared a number of times in Christian thought. St. Augustine, for example, had some rather negative things to say about the vanity and pride fostered by his boyhood study of the ancient Greek writings to the neglect of those that would foster love of God.[36] More to the point was the dilemma of certain Puritans. Will Herberg has pointed out that "the Puritans were not only the apostles of the Reformation, but also the heirs of medieval scholasticism and the humanistic Renaissance." The Reformation emphasis stressed that "the fundamental purpose of all human enterprises, including education, was to promote the Christian faith and advance the Christian life." Some Puritan leaders, such as John Winthrop, were disturbed by the prominence of the "pagan classics" at Harvard. This "Puritan problem," says Herberg, is seen in the fact that "whereas the purpose of Puritan education was Christian, its philosophy and psychology were humanistic, harking back to Athens rather than to Jerusalem."[37]

Sverdrup maintained that the Lutheran tradition out of which he had come contained a similar conundrum. He argued that theological education should be Christian in its fundamental assumptions. The "age of the congregation" demanded pastors whose training from beginning to end had been shaped by the understanding that comes from a thorough study of Scripture and church history rather than from immersion in the "pagan" classics. Seminarians should study those classics, but from a totally different vantage point.

Sverdrup's solution may not have been the best one to meet the challenges of an industrialized, urbanized society buffeted by the currents of the modern age. He was no doubt wrong in ascribing what he called humanism to some of those who differed with his outlook. It is clear that the program he championed did not become the norm for most Christian groups in twentieth-century America. It cannot be denied, however, that he raised important issues, and he did so with a clarity and a conviction that deserve to be acknowledged. Not even the passing of time can take from him the recognition due an incisive and creative thinker. The proper nature of theological education is still much debated. Sverdrup's views have contributed to the variety present in American Protestant seminaries.

Seven

The Sovereignty of the
Free and Living Congregation

Robert Michaelsen, a historian of religious developments in America, has stated that the immigrant minister "faced the task of maintaining sufficient contact with the old ways so as to preserve the roots of faith while also adapting his ministry to the new environment." As for the immigrant churches, Michaelsen says that their "fundamental problem was to distinguish between those cultural forms which were extraneous to the gospel . . . and those beliefs and practices which had to be preserved if the faith was to stand."[1] The tension between retention and preservation was also present within the larger Norwegian immigrant community. The differences of opinion over how the church should be governed—differences that surfaced again in the 1890s—can be considered part of that adjustment.

Over the centuries questions of church government, or church polity, to use the more technical term, have come to the fore with considerable intensity at times. Three basic positions—episcopal, presbyterian, and congregational—have developed, each with supporters who believed it to be divinely established. Such strong commitments to a given position have exacerbated the controversies among church bodies and peoples.[2]

The episcopal pattern—held in some form by the Roman Cath-

127

olic, Eastern Orthodox, Anglican (Episcopal), Methodist, and some Lutheran churches—emphasizes the office of the bishop as central to the nature of the church. A clear distinction is generally made between clergy and laity, with considerable control over church affairs placed in the hands of the clergy. Some of the churches following this pattern have developed a true hierarchy, with clearly defined ranks within the clergy.

The presbyterian structure, to which such groups as the Presbyterian and Reformed churches subscribe, emphasizes the authority of an elected body or bodies. Whether they are called councils, synods, sessions, consistories, or presbyteries, they are generally made up of both clergy and lay people. Such a structure enables the denominations that use it to exercise a measure of control and discipline over individual congregations and to promote united activities and concerns without the clerical dominance that they associate with the episcopal pattern.

The congregational polity—held by quite a number of groups in this country, including Congregationalists, Baptists, Disciples of Christ, and some Lutherans—insists on the autonomy of the local church, where final authority rests. It is a stance that clearly guards the rights and freedoms of the local body of believers; its critics regard it as less effective in promoting united action. The congregational pattern has been particularly important in America. Historian Stow Persons has called attention to the role of the New England Puritans in making congregationalism "the most characteristic form of religious institutional life in America." He further observes that churches of "episcopalian and presbyterian forms of polity were gradually forced to make appreciable concessions in practice, if not in form, to the spirit of congregational independence." Elements of Puritanism also contributed to the development of American civil government.[3]

Persons' comments suggest that in practice there have been attempts to adapt, modify, and even combine these forms of church government. In theory, however, a denomination is usu-

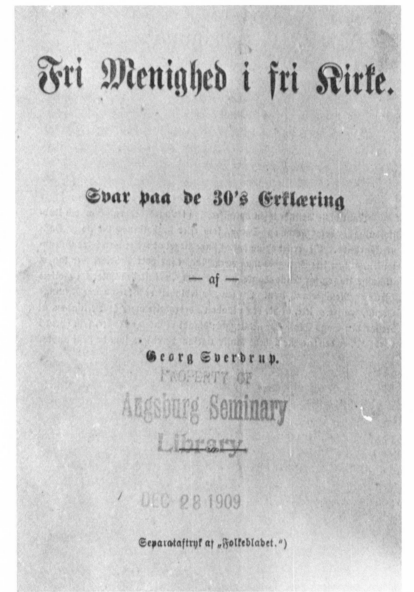

Title page of treatise indicating a central concern of Sverdrup's efforts in America: "a free congregation in a free church"

(Courtesy Augsburg College Archives)

ally committed to one or another of them. That commitment has sometimes been backed by the claim of divine sanction.

Historically, Lutherans have not regarded any particular form of church government as divinely established. Their confessional writings pointed to the pure teaching of the gospel and the proper administration of the sacraments as the two essential marks of the church. That has meant that from the Lutheran perspective the way in which the church is organized or structured is "subject to human insights and decisions; any polity is satisfactory as long as the two important marks are present."[4]

Such a stance has allowed for diversity in Lutheran church government. In some of the European countries where Lutheranism was established, including Scandinavia, there developed an episcopal pattern in which the highest civil official played a key role. These state churches not only operated with a clear distinction between clergy and laity, they also gave to the state an important role in running the affairs of the church.

Lutherans who came from such European countries found a very different environment in the United States. America's separation of church and state prohibited any type of state church. The Lutheran perspective on polity allowed them the flexibility to experiment. Perhaps inevitably, there were differences of opinion and clashes. Some favored a modified presbyterian pattern, in structures that attempted to balance congregational autonomy and control by a higher body. Others championed the decentralizing tendencies associated with congregationalism by putting more emphasis on the sovereignty of the local congregation. The debates of the 1890s in which Sverdrup was involved reflected such differences of opinion.[5]

It would be an understatement to say that the 1890 union did not work out as Sverdrup had hoped or anticipated. The Augsburg-St. Olaf controversy revealed differing and strongly held ideas of what theological education should be. In the heat of battle, these differences seemed insurmountable. The United

Church finally turned from Augsburg and established a divinity school at another location. Augsburg was left to work out its role outside the larger body. Augsburg's supporters believed these developments would enable the school to demonstrate the relevance of its educational principles to the preparation of pastors who would suit the democratic American context.

The experiences of the 1890s had a profound impact on Sverdrup. They brought into clearer focus his views on theological education as he sharpened his critique of "humanism" and was forced to explain what he meant by a "congregation-oriented education" (*menighedsmæssig præsteuddannelse*). They also led to a reassessment of aspects of his views on church government. The role of the individual congregation assumed a more dominant place in his writing and speaking, while the authority of the church body was specifically reduced. He came to reject any structure that gave considerable authority to the synod. In its place he substituted the congregational pattern as the one in accord with God's will.

An assessment of Georg Sverdrup must always take into account the fact that he came from a country with a state church. He retained throughout his life the conviction that the state church had stifled and suppressed the growth of the congregation as it was described in the New Testament. The zeal and determination with which he carried on his work reflected his belief that America offered a chance to correct the damage.

Even as a student in Norway Sverdrup had shown concern for questions of church government.[6] During his early years in America he had devoted considerable attention to such issues, for he believed that one of the most difficult tasks for a free church was to find the correct outer form to express the inner connection among congregations. Sverdrup's position prior to the difficulties of the 1890s might be described as one that combined elements from the presbyterian and congregationalist patterns. He wanted to guard against dominance by the clergy and to emphasize what he regarded as the proper role of the laity in congregational life. Thus he had championed the "free congregation" in his church body, the Conference. In his pre-1890 years he had viewed such congregational freedom in the context of a definite measure of authority given to the church body. He thought then that the church body too was meant to be free. During that period of his life Sverdrup saw this freedom properly expressed in the representative system. In one of his writings he stated it this way: "A free congregation in a free church means that the congregations are really represented at the annual meetings; that the decisions of the annual meeting really become an expression of the desires of the congregations; that the congregations, through their representatives at the annual meetings, deliberate, confer, and decide in such a way that no congregation needs to say no." He maintained that "by means of an equal and vigorous representation" there could begin to be "a free congregation in a free church."[7] In fact, at that time Sverdrup went so far as to say that the decisions of the annual meeting of the church body were "morally binding" on the congregations. "It is far too costly," he said, "for church bodies to hold annual conventions just to talk and give advice."[8]

Sverdrup had also expressed that point of view in the deliberations leading up to the union of 1890. Some persons had wanted to give the new church body only an advisory capacity in relation to the individual congregations. Sverdrup spoke against such a limitation of church authority, saying that he wanted nothing to do with such congregational "Copperheads."[9] After the 1890 union, however, Sverdrup's views changed over time under the pressure of concern for his school.

Augsburg had many supporters who felt that this school with its unique principles should be maintained. From their point of view, troubles arose because the majority within the new church had attempted to destroy the educational pattern that had been developed at the school. That majority, they felt, had no real appreciation of the fact that Augsburg had been designed to overcome the gulf between pastors and laymen. Augsburg supporters believed that they had been treated like immature children by the majority and that their proposals for resolving the impasse in a way that would safeguard Augsburg's role had not been given a chance to succeed.[10]

As early as 1893 these "Friends of Augsburg" (*Augsburgs Venner*) had begun to meet to consider how the school could be preserved. As a minority within the United Church, they felt that it was their duty to resist what they perceived as the high-handed methods of the majority. The reports from the meetings held by the Friends for several years convey the impression that they felt abandoned by the larger church body. The Friends were convinced that their principles were right and worth struggling for. Heroic efforts were therefore necessary to sustain the school. Eventually others too would recognize that that institution stood for something vital in the building of a free church in America.[11]

Although the Friends of Augsburg did not think of themselves as having separated from the United Church, they soon began to assume some of the functions of a distinct body. As early as 1893 they issued a report from the "Minority's Mission Committee" in which they urged taking steps to support those missionaries who shared their convictions. The next year the group constituted itself a "permanent organization" with a president and secretary. Sverdrup served as president of the Friends prior to their organization as the Lutheran Free Church in 1897. Soon there existed the machinery for supporting and promoting separate home and foreign missions, for ordaining candidates for the ministry who had been refused that rite by the United Church, and for propagating pro-Augsburg views through the pages of *Folkebladet*.[12]

Relations between the Augsburg faction and the majority within the United Church were further strained in 1895 and 1896. In 1895 Sverdrup and Oftedal had been chosen by Trinity Church in Minneapolis to be official delegates to the annual convention of the United Church. The church body refused to seat them. The United Church also suspended twelve congregations that had supported Augsburg and began legal action to gain control of Augsburg Seminary. All of these factors made it difficult to maintain the minority's façade as a continuing part of the larger church body.[13]

Out of these developments came Sverdrup's disenchantment with the representative system. One clear statement of that change is to be found in a series of articles in *Folkebladet* dealing with "the power of the church body and the free congregation." In them Sverdrup asserted that many persons had come to think that a church body, as one of the means by which God discloses his will, was something infinitely higher than the congregation. "The church is that mysterious, holy means through which God still reveals his will; the pastors are the servants of this body who descend from this great and exalted body to the small and impure congregations with commands." Sverdrup called this a "papistical" view of the church and said that there was always the danger that it could become dominant, even in America. He argued instead that the congregation was sovereign. The church body and the congregation needed to "exchange places," so that that which had been elevated would become a servant. Congregations could indeed co-operate in carrying out their objectives; they could even surrender some of their freedom to the authority of the church if they chose to do so. But everything had to be done in freedom and love. As for "the representative system," Sverdrup spoke of it now as "a Catholic invention." He was convinced that in the United Church that system had permitted a majority to exclude the minority, depriving that segment of the opportunity to promote its views. He felt that to permit only one side to champion its cause was a denial of freedom. He maintained that even "in the most corrupt political body it is considered inadmissible to crush the work of the minority by

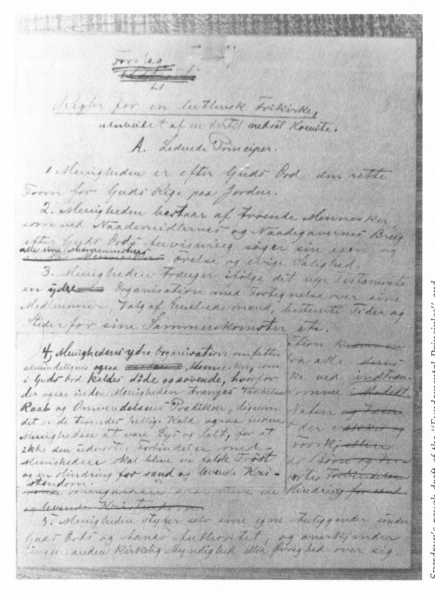

Sverdrup's rough draft of the "Fundamental Principles" and "Rules for Work" for a Lutheran Free Church
(Courtesy Augsburg College Archives)

driving it out and depriving it of the right to vote." And he was convinced that the United Church had done precisely that, demonstrating that it was not a truly free church.[14]

In 1896 the Friends of Augsburg elected a committee "to draft a set of principles and rules for carrying on the work which was devolving upon them." Sverdrup and Oftedal were the most influential members of that committee. Three conditions were placed on the group: full recognition of the freedom of the congregation; strengthening the influence of co-operative work; and no increase in the number of "party organizations." The last reference meant that the committee was not to form a new authoritative church body for promoting one point of view. The results of its work were the "Fundamental Principles" (*Ledende principer*) and "Rules for Work" that served to guide what came to be called the Lutheran Free Church, organized in 1897. Sverdrup said of these documents that they were not a proposal for a constitution but rules for co-operation to enable the congregations to answer their calling and fulfill their tasks. For the Lutheran Free Church was giving up the "often-misused representative system." It was not to be a new synod; it was conceived as a fellowship or association of congregations bound together by a spiritual rather than an external bond. Sverdrup saw it as an attempt to let the voluntary spirit rule. He also felt that the reorganization would make clear that the group was no longer simply a part of the United Church.[15]

The "Fundamental Principles," consisting of twelve statements, served as a basic document for expressing the outlook of the Lutheran Free Church. They also provide a convenient summary of Sverdrup's views on church government in his mature years, for not only was he a key figure in the drafting of the principles, he also provided a commentary on them in *Folkebladet* during 1898 and 1899.[16]

The first article, stating that the congregation is "the right form of the Kingdom of God on earth," is the key one. In his comments on it, Sverdrup maintained that the New Testament said nothing about an episcopate, papacy, church department, consistory, council, or synod over the congregation, but no other form of organization could be regarded as "a necessary part of Christianity." Sverdrup maintained that the Lutheran Free Church was working for "the restoration of the congregation in the biblical, and especially the New Testament, form."[17]

Sverdrup also used biblical imagery to support his contention that the congregation was the only divinely instituted form of the kingdom of God on earth. He noted that there were interpreters who would apply such expressions as "the body of Christ, the bride of Christ, God's living temple of living stones, God's people, and his abode in the Spirit" to the whole church only. Sverdrup rejected that interpretation. He maintained that "the congregation has everything that the church has and is everything that the church is."

He took the position that the congregation "directs its own affairs" and "acknowledges no other ecclesiastical authority or government above itself." The experiences of the 1890s had convinced Sverdrup and Augsburg's other supporters that the synodical pattern as they had experienced it in the United Church was as objectionable as a state church. In its place they affirmed a thoroughgoing congregationalism. This stance led John O. Evjen to characterize the Lutheran Free Church as "the only Lutheran body in America in which the congregationalist polity has been consistently carried through."[18]

Although Sverdrup believed the congregation to be "the right form of the kingdom of God on earth," his astuteness as a theologian kept him from simply identifying one with the other. Elsewhere he noted that "the kingdom of God" was a broader concept than the congregation. The congregation had an identifiable beginning—the Pentecost experience discussed in Acts 2, where the Holy Spirit is described as transforming Jesus' frightened band of followers into a witnessing community. The Kingdom

Spaulding lecturing to class in theology, 1907.

Augsburg faculty and students gathered for chapel services, 1897
(Courtesy Augsburg College Archives)

of God, however, encompassed also the many divine preparatory activities in the human race. Here Sverdrup was apparently referring to Old Testament accounts of divine workings among the Israelites and to God's dealings with humankind in general thereafter. It also included the many effects of the Christian revelation that existed alongside the congregation in such areas as "human cultural life, art, science, literature, [and] government." In a brief statement he described the relationship between the two in this fashion: the congregation is the central stream (*livsstrøm*) in the kingdom of God on earth.[19]

One might wish that Sverdrup had explored those ideas in greater detail, for his statement contains some intriguing hints of an interesting perspective on the relationship between Christianity and culture. Such an exploration also might have helped to alleviate the impression, noted earlier, of anti-intellectualism at Augsburg. Pietism, with which some "awakening" movements have been associated, has sometimes been portrayed as fostering an indifference to or neglect of cultural concerns in favor of the cultivation of the religious life. By developing this topic, Sverdrup might have added his voice to those who have demonstrated otherwise.

Another of the "Fundamental Principles" indicates that it is believers who make up the membership of God's congregation, defined as a reality consisting of people and of Word and sacraments. In that sense one could speak of "a visible congregation of believing people." Does that mean that the congregation is perfect, free from sin? That is, did Sverdrup share the view of some Puritans and certain other Christian groups that it would be possible to create a congregation of "visible saints"? The principles themselves and Sverdrup's commentary indicate that the answer is no.

The objective, of course, was always to work for a congregation in which there would be a gathering of "believing people." But Sverdrup shared the view of most Lutherans that there would be hypocrites in the organized congregation. He also stressed that the congregation "cannot judge the secret condition of the heart." The congregation could only take into consideration "the outward signs and marks of the . . . Christian life."[20]

It was precisely at that point that Sverdrup so often stressed the need for a "quickening preaching of the Word of God" to enable the congregation to "purify" itself. His goal was the creation of congregations that were "alive and free." There were some, he noted, who suggested that the way to achieve that objective was to separate believers from unbelievers. They advocated expelling the unbelievers in order to create a congregation of believers only. Sverdrup rejected that approach. Of prime importance to him was to work for "living" pastors with a "living" message. With such pastors there was at least a chance that the congregation would begin to come forth in its proper form. They would provide the "earnest admonition and exhortation" that would always be needed so long as the church existed in the world. His rejection of humanism in the education of pastors must also be seen in that context.[21]

The importance attached to the role of the pastor was not meant to imply that he alone worked to promote the Christian cause. According to another of the articles, all of "the spiritual gifts" were to be encouraged and used by everyone, not just by pastors and congregational officers. Not only should the congregation use the gifts that are found in it; "it is also incumbent upon the congregation to enliven, encourage, elicit, and call forth the gifts." Sverdrup related this emphasis on active service to continuous purification. He felt that if everyone were encouraged to be involved in spiritual work, the "worldly elements" in the congregation would find themselves quite cramped and would not be able to settle down in a "false security."[22] In this way the unbelievers would be induced to leave voluntarily the community of believers, or to become believers themselves.

The emphasis upon the sovereignty of the congregation did

141

not mean that it would exist in total isolation. Sverdrup repeatedly stressed the importance and necessity of "mutual assistance" in a number of areas of church work. As in most free-church movements, however, the operative term was "voluntary co-operation." The voluntary spirit would replace domination or coercion. Sverdrup once sought to make that distinction by referring to the two English words *co-operation* and *concentration*. Co-operation, he said, means that many forces work together because they have common interests. Concentration means that there is a central power leading the work because that is the only way to attain the greatest possible unity. A genuine free church, he said, operated on the basis of co-operation; a state church or a church body imbued with the high-churchly perspective sought to impose its will by concentration. Free co-operation could be achieved only by the assent of all who wished to join in the work. No congregation, leader, or agency for co-operative work could impose obligations on congregations or individuals not wishing to be a part of a given task. Sverdrup held that two great dangers threatening the development of church work in America were hierarchy and individualism. The only thing that could offer protection against them was restoration of free congregations that would associate with one another in Christian work. Here, then, was a clear statement of that voluntary principle that Winthrop S. Hudson called "the great tradition of the American churches."[23]

Co-operation also replaced union as an objective for Sverdrup concerning relations between church bodies. He came to feel that those who worked so zealously for union often practiced church politics, conveniently forgetting his own earlier intense involvement in the process. For example, he eventually interpreted the goal of the United Church as the union of all Norwegian Lutheran bodies in a form linking outer unity with majority rule. In opposition to that Sverdrup claimed that co-operation was a higher objective than external unity. Let those who are of the same spiritual outlook (*aandsretning*) join together in the tasks in which they have mutual interests, he suggested. Such an approach, he felt, would be far more productive of the desired results than would an outer unity brought about by political maneuverings.[24]

The rejection of the representative system had certain practical results. One example is seen in the provisions adopted by the Lutheran Free Church concerning the right to vote at its annual conference. The "Rules for Work" stated that that right was given to *all* voting members of Lutheran Free Church congregations who came to the meeting, as well as to voting members of other Lutheran congregations who would submit their names to the conference secretary by signing a statement indicating support of the Principles and Rules of the Lutheran Free Church. A representative church body in which there was the possibility of majority domination was to be replaced by a fellowship of sovereign congregations co-operating in mutual tasks. The change in theory necessitated a modification of voting practices.[25]

The decentralizing tendencies expressed themselves in other practical matters as well. The president of the Lutheran Free Church, for example, was elected for one year and could succeed himself only once. His responsibilities were restricted "chiefly to serving as moderator of the annual meeting." Further, independent boards and corporations were established to carry on the joint tasks of the congregations, with the annual meeting nominating candidates to them and receiving reports from them. Church historian Eugene L. Fevold alluded to one of the drawbacks of such a thoroughgoing congregationalism when he noted that this made it difficult for the Lutheran Free Church to marshal "its resources for cooperative work and in providing unified or integrated leadership for its activities." He further suggested that in the course of the twentieth century "many changes were made in the 'Rules for Work' and strong leadership emerged, which resulted in the Lutheran Free Church's functioning more and more like other Lutheran Synods." Some of the basic features of the early plan did, however, remain.[26]

Much of Sverdrup's writing in the years following the organization of the Lutheran Free Church focused on the congregation. Some of it tended to be polemical in nature, especially during the late nineties. The strained relations with the United Church had taken their toll on Sverdrup. They influenced his writings as he sought to explain and defend the positions of the Lutheran Free Church. One illustration of this tendency can be noted. In 1897 President Hoyme of the United Church had stated that that body was not searching for new ways: "The old means—Word and sacraments—and the old church order are good enough." Sverdrup picked up the expression "the old church order" and wrote a lengthy series of articles in *Folkebladet* to challenge that concept. He argued that "the old church order" had its origin in the state church. When transferred to America, it upheld the aristocracy of the ministerial office by church politics. In that pattern, he said, the pastor became separated from the people and the congregation. Sverdrup held that this old order produced a "form Christianity" which was the bitterest enemy of genuine spiritual life. He was convinced that it was necessary to break with "the old church order" so as to defeat such enemies as clerical dominance and worldliness. Sverdrup's articles conveyed the impression that the United Church, with its commitment to the old pattern, lacked a measure of the true spirituality that he felt was so desperately needed in America at that time.[27]

A strain in his relations with the United Church continued until his death in 1907, yet many of his writings from the early years of the twentieth century were more positive in nature. Perhaps the sharpness of the struggle of the earlier decade was forgotten somewhat as the work of Augsburg and the Lutheran Free Church settled into a more regular pattern. At any rate, he began to focus more on what needed to be done—and what avoided—in order to bring forth the ideal congregation. He never claimed that it was an easy task or one that he and the Augsburg supporters had accomplished, but he was convinced that it should be the main goal of Christian work. He also believed that the first Christians provided a model for later Christians to follow. His study of Luther also convinced him that his view of the congregation was supported by the Reformer. He believed that those who claimed to be Luther's followers should grasp the opportunity in America to restore this New Testament reality that had been distorted and "buried" for centuries, but he never urged his readers to forsake a congregation that did not meet his standards. If they should find themselves in such a situation, he counseled, they should devote themselves to patient prayer and work. Only in that way would a result that was constructive rather than destructive be brought to pass.[28]

Sverdrup's vision of an ideal congregation, one he described as "free and living," can best be defined as a living organism in which pastor and members worked together for their mutual edification and the spread of the Christian message. The congregation was not to be regarded as a mission field for the pastor; it was to be viewed as a functioning entity in which every member was enlisted in the tasks to be carried out. To sustain life it needed to be nourished by spiritual resources—Word and sacraments—rather than by "human reason or humanism or civilization." Sverdrup regarded the state church way as a compromise between the world and the church, while the free church way would seek to eliminate such compromises and strive to build the congregation to be a missionary force in the world. He once described the congregation as a reality independent of such conditions as ancestry, color, country, or language. It did not consist of a special class, age group, or educational level. It was rather made up of those who had separated themselves from the world and who endeavored together to upbuild one another and to spread the Christian message to all people.[29] To help achieve that goal among Norwegian immigrants was the point toward

145

which Sverdrup directed his energies. During the last ten years of his life he did so within the framework of the Lutheran Free Church.

Was Sverdrup's vision of a "free and living" congregation, as some of his admirers thought, the most profound interpretation of the Christian congregation since the time of the New Testament?[30] Such an assessment seems difficult to sustain. As noted, it was not without problems in terms of practical application. Further, Sverdrup's claim of divine sanction for his perspective— the view that the congregation was "the right form of the kingdom of God on earth"—digressed from the traditional open-ended stance of Lutheranism concerning church government. He was prepared to make absolute the pattern that he felt the New Testament, church history, and the experience of Christians in Norway and America had shown to be correct.

Yet his many statements on various aspects of the life of the congregation, usually addressed to specific needs or developments, indicated the work of an astute thinker. Had he been able to develop his insights in a comprehensive and systematic manner, it seems likely that he would have made a valuable contribution to ecclesiology, that area of theological consideration dealing with the nature of the church.

Even as it was, his contributions were useful. An observation by John O. Evjen points to the striking similarity between the "Fundamental Principles" of the Lutheran Free Church and certain documents from the Congregational Church. Evjen goes on to suggest that the history of the Lutheran Free Church, formed in its early years by Sverdrup and Oftedal, shows that the most widely diffused polity in Protestant North America—the congregationalist—is reconcilable with the spirit of the Lutheran confessional writings.[31] One may disagree with Sverdrup's claim of divine sanction for this arrangement; nevertheless, his efforts helped to demonstrate that Lutheranism could function within a fully congregational pattern.

One also sees here an interesting illustration of Sverdrup's openness to using American concepts. Immigrants differed in their responses to America. Sverdrup, while not an uncritical admirer of all phases of life in the New World, prized those elements that he felt enhanced freedom. He came to regard an association of free congregations as the structure that would best preserve the freedom of individuals and of the local body of believers. The pattern that had become so influential in America was one he sought to appropriate for Norwegian Lutheran immigrants.

.

Eight

The Fruits of Free-Churchly Work

The developments that led to the formation of the Lutheran Free Church meant that Sverdrup was identified for the rest of his life with a minority wing of Norwegian Lutheranism in America. The annual reports from the earliest years of the Lutheran Free Church did not include such items as number of congregations, total membership, or complete clergy rosters. They did, however, list the names of those attending the annual convention as pastors, professors, and lay persons. Some indication of size can be gathered from the fact that in the first years of the fellowship the number of pastors and professors in attendance ranged from sixty to eighty.[1] 1907 was the first year for which more complete statistics were given. That year "105 pastors reported for 283 congregations and eighty-one preaching places [locations where services were held, but which were not organized into congregations], representing 26,442 souls (baptized members)." In comparison with such bodies as the United Church and the Norwegian Synod, the Lutheran Free Church was considerably smaller.[2] Sverdrup's immediate sphere of influence, it can be noted, was at this point a fellowship roughly the size the Conference had been when he arrived in America in 1874.

But size was not Sverdrup's major concern. Far more important were the basic principles involved. The size of the Lutheran Free Church might not be great, but if its congregations were truly committed to the goal of a free church, then it would be a model for the other churches and for Christians in Norway who were struggling to be free of state control.[3]

As a response to a criticism that "the Free Church has good principles but doesn't practice them," Sverdrup wrote a series of articles in 1902 on the topic of "the principles of the Free Church in practice." Acknowledging that there might be an element of truth in that charge, Sverdrup faced it squarely and attempted to clear up misunderstandings about the implications of Free Church fundamentals. He wrote in some detail about how principles could and should be put into practice and what the benefits would be. He considered preaching that was "biblical, quickening, and edifying" to be of the first importance because it would have a strong influence on congregations beyond their required attendance at church services. This perspective stressed the importance of the pastor, whose primary task was not to "keep the machinery functioning" but to inspire people to give serious consideration to their relationship with God. Such preaching was seen as essential for the ongoing purifying of the congregation.[4]

Sverdrup, though not ordained, was often invited to preach and speak at church services and on special occasions. The many notes, outlines, and manuscripts for sermons and meditations that have been preserved testify to that fact. He also published in *Folkebladet* several accounts of speaking tours he had undertaken in the early 1880s, reports that include descriptions of terrain and people.[5]

One of these trips was to Illinois, where he had occasion to visit what he called "our oldest Norwegian settlement in America." His account described traveling by train through southern Minnesota and Iowa. Passage through Rock Island, Illinois, the location of the Swedish Augustana Synod Theological

Seminary, prompted these comments: "It is with unmixed joy that we look toward this center for enlightenment (*oplysning og aand*) . . . and we rejoice that the free people, in their love for God's Word and Christ's Church, can build just as good seminaries as the old coercive state churches. It almost appears as though the Lutheran church people from Sweden and Norway have accomplished as much in fifty years as the old countries did in 500."

The goal of that trip was the area near Morris, Illinois, a region of early Norwegian settlement that experienced, said Sverdrup, many of the divisive religious tendencies common among Norwegian immigrants. His trip included a visit to a Hauge's Synod congregation. He also spent some time with P. A. Rasmussen, a pastor of the Norwegian Synod, and wrote about the great hospitality with which Rasmussen received him. Their discussions reflected differences concerning how best to build a free church in this new land. Such differences—and Sverdrup's earlier-noted antipathy toward the general outlook of the Norwegian Synod—did not prevent acceptance and fellowship on a personal level.

Another of the *Folkebladet* accounts dealt with trips to what Sverdrup called "the Minnesota valley"—the area around Montevideo, Minnesota, in the west-central part of the state. He spoke in a number of immigrant churches in that area. His article provided an opportunity to note some of the difficulties settlers there had faced—the Dakota War in 1862, the memorable snowstorm of January, 1872, and the grasshopper plague of the years 1875–1877. He suggested that these difficulties also had a beneficial side: "the many indications of mature understanding of both temporal and spiritual matters indicate that sufferings and trials are a useful school for a person." He was also impressed by the beauty of the region. "A summer evening with the sunset's rich colors over the prairies and hills around the confluence of the Minnesota and Chippewa rivers at Montevideo is incomparable," he wrote. "The quiet peace and beauty of nature awaken reminders of paradise in the soul and put in the human heart a strange, blessed longing for the heavenly dwellings."

A third account dealt with a trip to northwestern Minnesota and North Dakota after the Conference's annual meeting in 1885. P. O. Strømme, a pastor and official in the Minnesota district of the Norwegian Synod, was also on the train. Sverdrup noted that there was soon good fellowship between Strømme and Conference representatives as they conversed about "the remarkable Minnesota district." Once again, personal relationships transcended some of the tensions between church bodies.

Sverdrup spent some days on that trip in churches in the vicinity of Crookston, Minnesota, before going on to North Dakota. He was impressed by the enormity of the prairie in both areas, but especially in North Dakota. He related it to the experience of the immigrants: "Poor Norwegian cotter, who has received 480 acres for almost nothing, who can wonder if you feel like a king every day of the year—unless it would be when a genuine Dakota blizzard makes it dark on the prairie in the middle of the day."

One can surmise that these speaking tours must have been demanding, since preaching must have been tiring, but it allowed Sverdrup to see and hear for himself what was happening in the churches of rural Norwegian America.

Sverdrup's preaching has been described as being "somewhat in the nature of a lecture." He conveyed the impression of giving instruction on something of real importance, an impression that made a strong impact on many of his hearers. That approach contrasted with a style of preaching that Sverdrup had noted in America. He once wrote that in this country there was no compulsion in church attendance, leading some clergy to feel that the sermon must attract people to church. The pastor's role was thereby reduced to that of gathering many people by "carnal eloquence." This led to preaching about social and political questions, with the sermon made as sensational as possible in order to attract large crowds of people. "The sermon must be pleasing in one manner or another so that listeners are attracted to the exciting or shocking 'entertainment'," Sverdrup claimed. He did not share that concept of preaching.[6]

Many who heard Sverdrup speak observed that his presentations were clear, logical, and delivered with authority.[7] The content of his messages emphasized such basic biblical themes as sin and grace, renewal and faith. He often drew a sharp contrast between the world and the life of following Christ. The Christian life was seen as a struggle, a battle in which Satan and the world would seek to lead one astray. Sverdrup's sermons were direct, addressed to the heart in an attempt to awaken the "sleeping, secure, worldly church members" and to call all Christians to "fight the good fight of faith" in a world that always sought to distract God's children from the narrow way. Sverdrup opposed what he regarded as form or mass Christianity and in his sermons made clear that being a Christian was not just being on the membership roster of a congregation. To him, it involved rather a living faith and a personal commitment to Christ.[8]

Some of Sverdrup's sermons from the 1890s contain nuances and overtones from the struggles of that period. He and Sven Oftedal published a book of their sermons, *Aand og liv* (Spirit and Life) in 1898. In them the congregation was portrayed as a little flock consisting of those committed to following Christ, often scorned and rejected by those who would follow the old ways which prevented the true freedom of the congregation. Individuals and congregations did not find release by means of rules and constitutions, Sverdrup asserted, but were set free by the work of the Spirit. It was the Spirit who created the bonds of fellowship that united individuals in a congregation and united congregations with one another, he believed.[9]

Earlier chapters have noted certain similarities between Sverdrup's stance and that of Grundtvig. It is tempting at this point to suggest that Sverdrup's outlook has some things in common with another noted nineteenth-century Danish thinker, Søren Kierkegaard. That influence could be seen in Sverdrup's distinguished professor, Gisle Johnson, who had been influenced by Kierkegaard, especially in his sharp criticism of the state church. It is true that Sverdrup, like Kierkegaard, opposed any presentation of Christianity that would allow persons to think they were Christians just because they lived in a Christian nation or went through the form of being Christian. Both men expressed negative sentiments about the state church, and both stressed the need for earnest commitment and dedication. Indeed, Sverdrup wrote of Kierkegaard as a "penetrating revivalist" (*skarp vækkelsesmand*) whose message had influenced an awakening in Norway. But Sverdrup also felt that Kierkegaard lacked an adequate concept of the Christian congregation, an omission with significant consequences.[10]

The possibility of some Kierkegaardian influence on Sverdrup cannot be excluded, but perhaps one is on safer ground if one sees in Sverdrup's preaching some of the themes associated with Norwegian pietism. The Haugean and Johnsonian awakenings had stressed a personal Christianity and the need for the Christian to be separated from "the world." Sverdrup linked these ideas with the concerns of the church reform movement and applied them to the situation of Norwegian immigrants in the New World as he understood it.

Encouraging lay activities was almost as vital to Sverdrup as preaching. His free-churchly principles stressed not only the pastor and the importance of correct ministerial education; they also made the point that the congregation must "practice" being the congregation. The pastor could point the way, but if a genuinely free and living congregation were to come forth, then all members had to take up their calling.[11]

The question of the proper role of lay activities—especially lay preaching—had been hotly debated in Norway. As noted above, the activities of Hans Nielsen Hauge had brought the issue to the fore during the early years of the nineteenth century. As a movement within the Norwegian state church, the Haugeans had stressed the validity of lay witnessing. Those who opposed such activities pointed to Article 14 of the Augsburg Confession, in which public preaching is limited to those who are "regularly called." Gisle Johnson's oft-noted "emergency principle," which restricted lay preaching to situations in which there was genuine need, was a compromise that did not please everyone. The controversy continued in Norway throughout much of the nineteenth century.[12]

As might be expected, Norwegian Lutherans in America also discussed the topic. In the years just prior to and during the Civil War, the Norwegian Synod considered it. In the deliberations leading up to the church merger of 1890, members of the Hauge's Synod worried that the other negotiating groups might not give proper recognition to the role of lay witnessing. The topic continued to be debated as several Norwegian-American Lutheran groups moved toward union in the early years of the twentieth century.

Georg Sverdrup repeatedly stressed the validity and the necessity of lay activity. He said that Norwegian lay activity had its origin in the religious experience in 1796 in which Hauge was called to be a witness to his people. In 1896, the jubilee year of that tradition, Sverdrup wrote an article in *Folkebladet* in which he spoke of the "inexpressible blessings for our people and our church" coming from lay activities. It was important, he said, for the whole church to go forth in Hauge's spirit.[13]

Not all Norwegian Lutherans in America fully shared Sverdrup's views on the matter, however. In 1895–1896 the tensions between the minority (the Friends of Augsburg, who were supporting the school, since by that time the United Church had established another seminary) and the majority in the United Church also were manifested in connection with lay activities.

The minority strongly emphasized the importance of such activities. Sverdrup maintained that the starting point in the discussion of revival and lay activities was that the one who had been brought to faith needed to proclaim his belief in the Savior and work for the salvation of others. All true Christians—men and women—had a duty to witness (*vidnepligt*) and a desire to see others saved from damnation. The only bounds to such activities were the limitations of individuals. Gifts of grace came from God's Spirit; thus it was the Spirit who impelled, led, and controlled lay activity. Where there was genuine revival, Sverdrup stated, there would be lay witnessing.

Objections to Sverdrup's views were forthcoming. Those who offered such criticisms were not necessarily opposed to lay activities as such, but they suggested that Sverdrup's emphasis on lay witnessing would deprive pastors and congregations of the necessary control of such activities, that it would permit sectarian or false prophets to function, and that it was contrary to Paul's New Testament admonition to do things in an orderly manner.

In responding to those criticisms, Sverdrup said that right-thinking pastors and congregations would encourage and participate in these spiritual efforts rather than be concerned about controlling them. The fact that there were false lay preachers should not be used as an argument to restrict or forbid those who were truly moved by the Spirit. In fact, said Sverdrup, the way to inhibit the work of false sectarian lay preachers was to follow the example of the apostolic congregations and Hauge's friends in Norway: people who did not belong to a congregation would not be accepted as speakers at church services. A congregation should welcome only those lay preachers who had good recommendations from respected Christians, and if pastors and congregations fostered genuine lay work, there would be no room for rootless false prophets. As far as control was concerned, Sverdrup stressed that the gifts of the Spirit were given for edification, "and we use them for that." He saw nothing contrary to good order in an active program of lay witnessing.[14]

Sverdrup noted that some people believed lay activities to be a threat to pastors. He acknowledged that problems could arise if the people in a congregation wanted lay witnessing while the pastor opposed it, but his basic point was that lay activities posed no threat to the pastor's work or honor. The work was so vast that all energies were needed. He compared the pastor to an officer in the army: it is best to have soldiers who are awake when the enemy attacks.

To the question, what should "the believers" (*de troende*) do in a situation in which the pastor and a majority in the congregation oppose lay activities, Sverdrup answered that they should meet for mutual encouragement and strengthening. They could also invite outsiders to join them, but since the opposition was often bitter, the outsiders had to be chosen with care. Sverdrup suggested that a committee might best lead the extra-congregational meetings.

Sverdrup also raised the issue of how to respond to those congregations in which "pure doctrine" served as a barrier and no lay activity of any kind was wanted. He posed the question: should authentic traveling lay preachers not respect congregational decisions and pastoral orders and stay away from such places? His answer was a decisive no. He noted that Hauge did not stay away just because he was not wanted. He contended that people who attempted to use pastors and worship as a barrier against authentic Christianity must not be allowed to do so, for they, too, needed to hear the voice of admonition. In fact, Sverdrup considered it more important to bear witness in congregations where the church doors were locked to lay preachers or where pastors regarded lay activities as sinful than to do so in other places. He did not state specifically how such activities were to be carried out. Presumably he felt it could be done without creating such controversy that the desired goal was made unattainable.[15]

Sverdrup thought a true congregation was a fellowship of working Christians who used the means and gifts of grace for

157

the salvation and edification of themselves and humanity. In such a context there would be no attempts to restrict and control lay activities and other gifts of grace. The emphasis would rather be on allowing room and freedom for the full exercise of such gifts. Such an emphasis, Sverdrup maintained, was not "foolishness," "fanaticism," or "ecclesiastical anarchy"; it was a kind of Christianity in which all of God's gifts were utilized for the spread of his kingdom.

PROMOTER OF THE DEACONESS MOVEMENT

Sverdrup included charitable activities among the positive fruits of free-churchly labor. One such activity to which he devoted considerable energy was the deaconess work that was organized in Minneapolis.

The term deaconess has been defined by one source as "a Christian woman called, trained, and set apart . . . for a full-time ministry of redemptive, loving service." The roots of the diaconate—an order of such women committed to works of charity and mercy—are found in the New Testament and in the early centuries of the Christian church. Various sources from those times indicate the existence of women within the Christian community, referred to as deaconesses, whose role was to serve those in need. However, with "the development of the ecclesiastical hierarchy and the withdrawal of devout persons into cloistered communities [the monastic movement] during the Middle Ages, the diaconate for women gradually waned until it disappeared from the life of the church."[16]

Among Protestants the restoration of a diaconate took place primarily in the nineteenth century. Sverdrup regarded the deaconess movement as a product of the religious awakening of that century. In response to the social conditions and needs of the time, Theodor Fliedner, a Lutheran pastor in Germany, established in the 1830s an association and training center for Protestant deaconesses. From there the movement spread to other lands, including the Scandinavian countries. In the United States,

William Passavant of Pittsburgh, a theologian and churchman belonging to the Lutheran synod called the General Council, was instrumental in promoting the cause among Lutherans.[17]

Lutheran deaconesses in the United States generally were affiliated with a "motherhouse," the institution in which they received their training. From there they might be sent to carry out their work in hospitals, children's homes, congregations, or in foreign missions. They could return periodically to the motherhouse for renewal, and it might serve as their home when they were old. Deaconesses, who received enough money to pay for their upkeep, generally wore a distinctive garb. Although they were referred to as "sisters," they were not bound by life-long vows and were free to leave the role if they chose. In an age when private charity was more important in meeting human needs than is the case in the latter part of the twentieth century, deaconesses were viewed as an important contribution churches could make to alleviating distress. Women were considered especially well suited to charitable and compassionate work. The specific motivation for service as deaconesses was seen as rooted in the Christian message.

The young women who chose to become deaconesses did need training, however. To that end Sverdrup regarded a deaconess home as essential. Such a place should be a school and a hospital, as well as a home for the sisters. It needed to be a school so that the deaconesses could be instructed in Scripture and trained for their special service to the needy. It should be a hospital so that the young women could gain practical experience in serving the sick. And it should provide a home atmosphere in which the deaconesses could share their joys and sorrows as they fulfilled their calling. Deaconesses were undertaking a special role in the church; only if they were properly educated could the church and society gain the greatest benefit from their work.[18]

The Norwegian Lutheran deaconess home in Minneapolis grew out of an 1888 gathering. In the fall of that year the General Council had met in the city. Passavant and Adolph Spaeth, both prominent General Council pastors, were among those invited to the home of Pastor M. Falk Gjertsen of the Norwegian-Danish Conference to discuss how to begin deaconess work. The first step was to obtain the services of a deaconess. This occurred soon after the meeting, when a deaconess from New York came to Minneapolis and agreed to undertake the task. The project soon foundered, however, and it appeared that it would come to naught. It was at that point, in August, 1889, that Sverdrup stepped in and organized a new board. A corporation was formed under the name of Norwegian Lutheran Deaconess Institute, and Sverdrup was elected president of the board. He served in that position until 1903. The writers of a historical sketch of the deaconess home and hospital have stated that while Sverdrup "was not, strictly speaking, the originator of the deaconess movement in the Northwest, he took charge of affairs when the cause seemed lost."[19]

Once established on a firm footing, the deaconess home and the cause were earnestly promoted and supported by Sverdrup. He lectured on deaconess work at the first convention of the United Church in 1890. During the summer of 1891 he and Professor M. O. Bøckmann of the United Church visited many congregations to gather funds and stimulate interest and understanding of the movement. He wrote a number of articles in *Folkebladet* explaining deaconess work and appealing for support, especially from congregational women's organizations.

By the 1890s many of the Norwegian Lutheran immigrant congregations had established active women's auxiliary groups (*kvindeforeninger*). These organizations often had a dual role: they raised money for congregational projects, and they tried to meet some of the religious and social needs of immigrant women. Sverdrup felt that deaconess work might have a special appeal to such groups, if he could make clear what the role involved. He and others also taught courses in religion to the young women being trained as deaconesses. His second wife, Elisa, who had been a deaconess at the government hospital in Oslo, taught deaconess work and nursing at the Minneapolis institution.

In 1898 Sverdrup's translation from German to Norwegian of Emil Wacker's book on the past and present work of the diaconate was published. All profits from the sale of the book went to the Minneapolis deaconess home. Sverdrup believed that all the Norwegian Lutheran churches in America should support this undertaking, since it had nothing to do with the strife among the synods.[20]

The result of the efforts of Sverdrup and others was a viable institution in Minneapolis—the Norwegian Lutheran Deaconess Institute (the name changed in 1923 to the Lutheran Deaconess Home and Hospital)—that provided deaconesses for service in the church at home and in foreign missions. During the early 1890s the United Church was a strong supporter of the institution. Following the formation of the Lutheran Free Church in 1897, however, much of its support came from that group; the Deaconess Institute came to be regarded as affiliated with that church body.

Sverdrup maintained that deaconess work was another means for furthering the great cause of a free church: the restoration of the congregation to its apostolic form (*menighedens gjenopreisning til dens apostoliske skikkelse*). Again, the congregation needed the freedom to use all of God's manifold gifts to his church. In the somewhat restricted nineteenth-century view Sverdrup shared, some gifts seemed especially suited for men, others for women. He described deaconess work as the church's utilization of the special gifts and abilities of women in Christian acts of love.[21]

Sverdrup noted that some people objected to the idea of a special order of deaconesses as something Roman Catholic, especially since the sisters wore a special garb. Their life style also suggested to some the Catholic approach of earning salvation through "good works." In responding to those objections Sverdrup said that the sisters wore a special dress because of their unique work. The garb served as a uniform and, like that of a soldier, identified a deaconess with her cause. As for "good works," he held that Lutherans certainly stressed them as the fruits of faith. We do not, said Sverdrup, seek to earn salvation by good works, but deaconess work was one of the ways in which Christian love could be expressed. Sverdrup contended that preaching the gospel and healing diseases went hand in hand during Jesus' life on earth and that the same should be true of his body, the church.

The development of interest in deaconess work among the Norwegian Lutheran immigrants took place at roughly the same time as the expression of what is called the "social gospel" within a number of Protestant denominations in America. The rise of large industrial centers had changed a number of facets of life in America. Reacting against the individualistic focus of early-nineteenth-century pietistic and evangelical Protestantism, and questioning the tendency to give religious sanction to the acquisitive spirit—as in such writings as Andrew Carnegie's "Wealth"—the proponents of the social gospel gave voice to a new concern for justice and the Christianizing of the social order. Their concern found expression in programs and institutions designed to assist those who lived in slums or in blighted industrial centers.[22]

Sverdrup is not to be numbered among the advocates of a social gospel in the strictest sense of that term. What his efforts on behalf of deaconess work suggest, however, is that he saw a clear link between the Christian message and works of mercy. He regarded the practice of this form of charitable work as a way of restoring to the congregation some of the vitality of the first Christian community.

Missions and the Free Congregation

Sverdrup's interest in mission work, noted earlier, continued throughout his life. He worked hard to generate the commitment and support that he felt it deserved. Sverdrup considered interest in evangelism—both at home and abroad—an essential mark of an emancipated and vital congregation.

Church historian Kenneth Scott Latourette wrote that "the 1790s and the opening years of the nineteenth century have generally been counted as seeing the beginning of the Protestant foreign missionary enterprise." Linked with some of the renewal of revival movements of that time, Protestant missionary societies came into being in Europe and the United States.[23]

This mission effort can also be related to Western colonialism or imperialism. Beginning as early as the fifteenth century, colonialism reached its peak during the nineteenth century, when Western influence was felt in Asia, Africa, and the Americas. The establishment of colonies was often accompanied by attempts to bring Christianity to the people in those regions, but the relationship between colonialism and the missionary enterprise was not always harmonious. As church historian James Hastings Nichols has stated, the "missionary impetus was sometimes aided and sometimes hindered by Western imperialism." Its central motive was to reach people with the gospel; at times that conflicted with the objectives of those seeking colonies.[24]

Interest in foreign mission work developed in Norway near the middle of the nineteenth century. Sverdrup pointed to the formation of The Norwegian Mission Society (Det norske Missionsselskab) in Stavanger in 1842 as an expression of that interest. He regarded it as one of "the many blessed fruits" of the Haugean movement. The Society established mission work in South Africa in the 1840s and in Madagascar in the 1860s.

Before 1890 foreign mission interest among Norwegian Lutherans in America had been channeled through the Norwegian Mission Society. Missionaries J. P. Hogstad and E. H. Tou may serve as examples of how this arrangement worked. After receiving their theological educations at Augsburg, they were sent to

Madagascar in 1887 and 1889 under an agreement with the Norwegian Mission Society. Their financial support came from Norwegian-American congregations.[25]

The creation of the United Church in 1890 led to the desire for an independent foreign mission field. Sverdrup and Pastor P. A. Rasmussen were chosen to go to Norway in 1892 to further the cause. Sverdrup was not able to go, but he was gratified when he received a telegram from Rasmussen announcing that an agreement had been worked out. The Norwegian Mission Society granted Norwegian Lutherans in America the southern portion of Madagascar as their own area of operation. Missionaries Hogstad and Tou thereafter came under the jurisdiction of the United Church. Not surprisingly, the tensions within the United Church in the 1890s affected foreign mission work. As the Friends of Augsburg found themselves more and more isolated, Hogstad and Tou cast their lots with that group. By 1895 the Friends had set up the machinery for supporting the missionaries. Thus when the Lutheran Free Church was formed in 1897, it already had established foreign missions in Madagascar.

As he did with the deaconess movement, Sverdrup took an active part in the mission effort. He served on the Board of Foreign Missions, which became the Lutheran Board of Missions after its incorporation in 1899. Sverdrup chaired the board the year it was incorporated; for the remaining years of his life he served as its secretary. The board's reports reveal the needs, achievements, and problems of the Madagascar missions. A number of them reflect a note of sadness as they discuss the illnesses and deaths resulting from living in an unaccustomed climate, but through all of them can be found Sverdrup's insistence on the necessity of preaching the gospel to the "heathen." He believed that work in foreign countries should follow the same basic pattern as at home: a focus on congregation, school, and charitable activities. The reports also show that Sverdrup was interested in and informed about the details of mission work in Madagascar.[26] Sverdrup's active participation is also seen in his service as the first editor of *Gasseren* (The Malagasy), a monthly magazine started to stimulate and sustain interest in missions. He was editor of the periodical from 1900 until his death in 1907.[27]

When the Lutheran Free Church was formed, Sverdrup wrote that its intention was to turn in all things from the methods used by the "majority" church body (which he felt involved compulsion) to the freedom of the apostolic congregation. This was to be true also in matters of mission work. The congregation, he stressed, was both the child of missions and the mother of missions; where there was truly a congregation there would be mission.[28]

Sverdrup's attempt to distinguish the methods of the Free Church from those of the United Church (the "majority" church body) seems overdrawn and reflective of the tensions of the 1890s. Those in the United Church concerned with missions, it can be argued, operated from motives and with methods more positive than Sverdrup suggested. What was distinctive about Sverdrup's emphasis, however, was his insistent demand that concern for mission be rooted in the enlivened and emancipated congregation he was striving to bring into being.

Sverdrup had always considered mission work vital to the church. In 1895 he described a genuine "mission sense" (*missionssans*) as the situation in which the one who had himself been saved sought the salvation of others. Christianity, he asserted, was not a collection of theoretical truths, but God's kingdom on earth, a gospel of God's love encompassing the whole human race.

That emphasis was still strong in a lecture he gave in 1906 on "the significance of missions for the congregation." In it he stated that mission was not simply one virtue among several, all more or less necessary for the committed Christian. It was rather an essential and unique expression of the life of God's Spirit as manifested in and through the congregation. Mission had to be a central concern (*hovedsag*) for the congregation, Sverdrup asserted, for no one could have the spirit of truth without wanting to share it. Sverdrup subscribed to the general idea of mission work, as expressed by him in pious terms: the gospel was entrusted to the congregation, not to enable the congregation to possess the message for itself, but so that it could allow the light to shine both at home and abroad. Sverdrup believed that God's kingdom was a victorious, conquering kingdom, but that it had to win without sword and bloodshed. Nor should mission work be undertaken to enhance the power of the church. Its sole aim should be to spread God's kingdom, said Sverdrup, for God wanted all people to be saved. His will would be fulfilled through the congregation's mission work. Mission therefore became an essential element in the life of the Christian congregation.[29]

Sverdrup also saw an ecumenical significance in mission work, noting that it often brought one into contact and sometimes into co-operation with distinguished Christian men and women of different confessions. One result, he held, was that greater emphasis was placed upon those essential beliefs held by all evangelical Christians, while the differences among them were of necessity subordinated. This led to greater simplicity in preaching and to greater mutual accord among Christians.[30]

It is of interest to relate Sverdrup's views at this point to certain tendencies in nineteenth-century American Lutheranism. One approach, which can be identified with S. S. Schmucker of Gettysburg Seminary (a school of the Lutheran body called the General Synod), emphasized the essential teachings held in common by all evangelical Christians. That outlook urged such Christian groups to regard one another as branches of the church of Christ and to co-operate where possible, even while remaining in their separate denominations. Another approach, with the Missouri Synod's C. F. W. Walther as a leading exponent, put much greater emphasis on the distinctively Lutheran teachings embodied in the Lutheran confessional writings; apart from doctrinal agreement, it was wary of co-operation with other Christian groups. Many of the tensions in nineteenth-century American Lutheranism reflected these divergent tendencies.[31]

These differences were manifested also among Norwegian Lutherans in America. The Norwegian Synod, for example, reflected some of the outlook of the Missouri Synod. Sverdrup, on the other hand, was among those who inclined toward Schmucker's position, which saw in mission work an opportunity to explore more common ground. Although it was affected by the tensions with the United Church, mission work also provided a place where the Lutheran Free Church and the United Church could co-operate. In the early 1900s, for example, it seemed wise to leaders of both churches, including Sverdrup, to exchange certain mission stations on Madagascar so that both would have more unified fields.[32]

With missions, as with deaconess work, Sverdrup's overarching interest was in the contribution they could make to the development of the new and vital congregation, the cause to which he devoted his career.

EPILOGUE

Nine

Home—Family—Friends

The discussion of Georg Sverdrup in preceding chapters has been directed toward an understanding of the prominent role that he played in religious developments among Norwegian Lutheran immigrants. By his teaching, writing, and speaking, he labored to create the type of educational and theological atmosphere that he felt was most suited to the democratic American environment. Sverdrup was not only a religious leader, thinker, and controversial figure, he was also a family man who appreciated the value of home and friends. The picture presented here would be incomplete without some reference to that dimension of his life.

Georg Sverdrup was married twice. His first wife was Cathrine (Katharina) E. Heiberg, daughter of a merchant from Bergen. She and Georg were married on June 25, 1874, when she was twenty years old, he twenty-five. That same summer they sailed for America, arriving in August in Minneapolis, where she took up her role as wife of a theological professor in what was then a small city in the Midwest. Such terms as quiet, unostentatious, and kind have been used to describe her.[1]

Georg and Cathrine Sverdrup came to Augsburg Seminary from Norway at the same time as Sven and Elise Gunnersen.

The handwritten memoirs of Elise Welhaven Gunnersen provide an interesting account of their trip to Minneapolis and allow some glimpses into the experiences of the seminary professors and their families during the 1870s and early 1880s. Elise told of a boat trip that lasted some three to four weeks, partly because of stormy weather and a delay caused by an explosion on the ship when a steam pipe ruptured. She noted their arrival in New York, where arrangements had been made for the two couples to stay in a hotel. The hotel was, from Mrs. Gunnersen's perspective, quite unsatisfactory, and the travellers did not remain long in New York. They journeyed by train, first to Pittsburgh and then to Chicago, where they were met by the prominent Scandinavian intellectual Rasmus B. Anderson, professor at the University of Wisconsin in Madison. They spent a short time in Chicago, seeing some of the sights in the company of Anderson. A train trip to Minneapolis finally brought them to their destination.[2]

Arrival in Minneapolis necessitated further adjustments to a new environment. Mrs. Gunnersen indicated that the two couples were brought to Augsburg Seminary, only to be told by Sven Oftedal (who had come the previous year) that the house that was supposed to be provided for them had not yet been built. Temporary quarters were established in the seminary building. After several weeks of construction, the house was ready for occupancy. It was in such a situation, at a date when there were still expanses of prairie quite near the Augsburg campus, that the new arrivals began life in America. Living so near one another enabled these seminary families to enjoy one another's company, but it also at times led to irritations and misunderstandings.[3]

Seven children were born to Georg and Cathrine Sverdrup. The oldest was Karl Ulrik, born in 1875. A second son, Andreas, lived only a few months. Else Magdalene grew up and married the Reverend Michael B. Michaelsen. George, the third son, became president and professor at Augsburg Seminary in 1911, several years after the death of his father. He continued in that role until his own death in 1937. Inga became the wife of Professor William Mills of Red Wing, Minnesota. Gunhild married Dr. L. N. Berg of Montevideo, Minnesota. Ragna Marie, the last child of this marriage, served as treasurer at Augsburg for many years.[4]

In 1887 typhoid struck the family. It took the life of Cathrine, who was not quite 34 years old, and of the oldest child, Karl Ulrik, aged twelve. Several of the other children were also affected by it and hovered for a time between life and death. During that troubled period a colleague described Sverdrup as "bent down with sorrow and worn out by the lengthy nightwatches and concern for the suffering children." He went on to observe that Sverdrup nevertheless carried out his tasks as teacher and president at the seminary with his "usual faithfulness."[5]

After the deaths of his wife and eldest son, Sverdrup was left with the care of five children. A relative from Oslo came to the United States to keep house for him during the period he was a widower.[6] In 1890 he married again. His second wife was Elisa Susanne Heiberg, a younger sister of Cathrine. She came to Minneapolis and was married to Georg on August 25, 1890. Elisa, who was 25 years old at the time, had served as a deaconess in Norway. She continued her interest in that work by teaching courses at the Deaconess Institute that had been established in Minneapolis by her husband and other Norwegian Lutherans. Two sons—Harald Ulrik and Edvard Fredrik—were born to them. Harald was a teacher in Los Angeles for a time and also worked for a lumber company in Alaska. Edvard worked as a chemical engineer in Buffalo, New York, and directed a laboratory in Mississippi. In 1904 Elisa became quite ill and there was fear that she would lose her life. She recovered, however, and lived until 1942. Andreas Helland described her as one who "lived to serve" and indicated that her "quiet, inconspicuous ministrations" helped many people.[7]

Georg and Elisa (Heiberg) Sverdrup. Children: (back row) Inga, Else, George; (front row) Ragna, Harald, Gunhild
(Courtesy George M. Sverdrup)

Sverdrup's concern for his family is reflected quite clearly in the rather extensive exchange of letters from the early 1900s between him and his son George. Some date from George's years at Yale, and others from his fellowship period in the Middle East.[8] In this correspondence the father wrote in Norwegian, the son in English. One area of deep concern in 1904–1905 was Elisa's health. In a letter from October, 1904, for example, Georg wrote to his son that "Elisa is sick, and it appears quite possibly that she is dying." George responded by saying, "I can't say how sorry I was to hear the sad news about mother and I hope that it can not be as bad as you seemed to think." By March of the next year Georg could write to his son that "it looks a little better with Elisa now. The doctor has abandoned his tuberculosis-theory and her condition is on the whole somewhat more satisfactory." He went on to say he hoped to be able to take her to their summer cottage when the weather warmed up, even though at the time she was still confined to bed. In letters from the summer of that year he expressed joy that Elisa was improving, was able to join in fishing, and could do some work around the house.

Many of these letters also contain references to ways of obtaining money for George to carry on his graduate studies at Yale and in the Middle East. The son often inquired about or referred to tutoring jobs, a scholarship or fellowship that might be available, borrowing money, and the like. The father, while indicating at times that his own resources were limited and needed for other things, was genuinely interested in these matters and expressed a willingness to help where possible. Georg clearly wanted his son to be able to take advantage of those opportunities that would equip him to serve effectively, and he dealt with these financial concerns with respect and patience.

Some of the letters discuss George's courses and research, including issues of biblical criticism and inspiration. For example, in a letter written in 1901, Georg encouraged his son to study Hebrew and Arabic, but also observed that the main issue was to grasp the "red thread" that runs through history and humanity so that there would be clarity and one could see the interconnectedness of the whole. In another letter from the same year he spoke of the necessity of dealing with questions of the Bible's inspiration and related issues. He went on to say, however, that in a certain sense these questions were insurmountable by scientific study (*videnskaben*), for it could deal only with externals. He also expressed the opinion that the conception of the Old Testament then fashionable would not maintain its credibility. "That type of hypothesis comes and goes," he observed. And yet he did not dismiss it as of no value: it could help to "shed light on one detail or another belonging to the main issue." The father was clearly interested in the questions his son faced as he confronted a new approach to the Scriptures. Georg's responses reflected a desire to be helpful without being dictatorial. His cautious openness to the new methodology allowed the son to wrestle with the issues on his own terms.

In later letters, after George had gone to the Middle East, Georg expressed considerable interest in the migration of Jews to Palestine (the Zionist movement). He felt the development was of great significance for religion and he encouraged his son to find out as much as possible about it.

This father-son exchange of letters also reveals that Georg maintained his scholarly interests throughout his life. In 1903, for example, when George indicated his intention to study Arabic and Syriac, Georg wrote that he had two grammar books on those languages, both written in German, and offered to send them to George. In the same letter he made a request of his son: "if you should find a *complete* [underlining in original] translation of Hammurabi's Inscriptions, let me know of it." Later he thanked George for some information on Hammurabi's "Code of Laws," saying that it was of great interest—especially if Hammurabi had lived during Abraham's era, as some scholars suggested. In a later letter Georg asked George to check the library at Yale for a scholarly book that had been published in Paris in 1867. He asked George to see whether it was as interesting and valuable as he had heard: "I have often thought of buying it, but out here we don't have the opportunity to see what we buy, and thus we often waste our money." In 1905, when he learned that George was going to Beirut, Georg wrote of the appeal of spending some time in the region "from which our religion and our civilization have come." He went on to speak of how "indescribably impressive" it is for the mind to be in this classical environment that contributed so much to the world's leading ideas.

Several letters to Georg from his mother and siblings in Norway have also been preserved. In 1900, for example, his mother sent a letter that she intended as a birthday greeting. She spoke of his work for "living Christianity" and of her joy that her son labored for that cause. She signed it "your old mother" (*Eders gamle Moder*). In 1903 came a telegram telling of her death, followed by a letter from his brother Harald that spoke in more detail about her death and funeral. Other letters from brothers and sisters kept him informed of what was going on among family members in Norway and inquired about the relatives in America. These letters, all from the early 1900s, indicate that Georg maintained contact with and was interested in his roots in Norway.

Georg Sverdrup's children and their descendants in the United States have gone into various professions and occupations in which they have made useful contributions to church and society. Among their roles have been clergy spouse, seminary president and professor, university professor, teacher, doctor, nurse, scientist, and business person. They are another means by which the Sverdrup name and influence have been felt in America. A family with roots in and continued links to Norway, it has also realized Georg's idea that it become a genuine part of this new land. In 1874 Georg Sverdrup came to America and spoke of it as "the land of the future." To this country he contributed not only his views on the congregation and theological education, but also a name that has appeared frequently among his offspring. His son was not the only one to be named George. A look at a list of descendants reveals that the name has been borne by grandsons, great-grandsons, and great-great grandsons. It is another way in which a distinguished ancestor continues to be remembered.[9]

Sverdrup's relationships and contacts with persons outside of his immediate family also provide insights into the nature of the man. This is especially true of his relations with his Augsburg colleagues, S. R. Gunnersen and Sven Oftedal. Sverdrup, Oftedal, and Gunnersen, it will be remembered, had been referred to as "the new triumvirate" at Augsburg. The three had been friends in Norway and shared similar views. All came to America as young men to work for the fulfillment of their goals, but after several years the relationship between Gunnersen and the other two no longer seemed to be as close as it had been. Elise Gunnersen stated in her memoirs that her husband tended to identify more with the "old direction" represented by August Weenaas, while Sverdrup and Oftedal were the leading spokesmen for the "new direction" in the Conference. She indicated that these differences were at times reflected in rather intense faculty meetings. Her assessment was that her husband lacked the charm of Oftedal or the wit and fluency in discussion of Sverdrup, even though in theological knowledge she regarded him as far superior to Oftedal and equal to Sverdrup except in Hebrew. She regarded Sverdrup and Oftedal as men who were able to get people to follow them, an ability her husband did not possess to the same degree. The strain in relations among the three Augsburg professors was most evident when Gunnersen resigned from his post at the seminary in 1883 and returned to Norway a year later. The breach was not permanent, however, for the friendship was restored through letters, and Sverdrup's published writings contain no negative references to Gunnersen. Sverdrup valued cordial personal relations even with people who did not share all of his views.[10]

Sverdrup's friendship and close working relationship with Oftedal continued throughout his life despite their very different personalities. Oftedal has been characterized as a gregarious, cosmopolitan figure who "would fit into any gathering." Another description suggests that "politics rather than teaching theology would have been more suitable to this dynamic, aggressive man who could move with equal ease in aristocratic or democratic circles." Theodore Blegen described Oftedal as "an orator and scholar feared for his wit and admired for his versatility, a student of many languages, including Greek, ancient and modern, and one of the builders of the Minneapolis Public Library system." Sverdrup, on the other hand, was a quiet man, possessing a reserve that "forbade familiarity." At times he gave the appearance of being cold and unsympathetic, but that should not be taken to mean that it was difficult to be in his company. John H. Blegen, who taught for a number of years in Augsburg's college-level department, described Sverdrup as "a pleasant person to have as a guest, neat and orderly in bearing, rich in knowledge and interesting in conversation, a man one could respect." It seems clear that Sverdrup was considerably less outgoing than Oftedal.[11]

Nevertheless, throughout their years together at Augsburg the relationship between them was close and cordial. Elise Gunnersen observed in her memoirs that the two men loved, respected, and admired each other. She also felt that there was some competition for first place between them, but that both recognized that they needed one another to achieve their goals in America. They visited frequently in each other's homes and held similar views on theological education, congregational freedom, and the need for a revitalized Christianity. Living in such close proximity enabled them to have frequent contact. Andreas Helland has written that Oftedal would often "ring the door bell" at nine o'clock in the evening, "and the two friends would find worthwhile relaxation in conversing about matters of common interest." When Cathrine Sverdrup died in 1887, Oftedal cut short his stay in Germany, where he had gone for his health after receiving a leave of absence from teaching. He returned to Minneapolis to assist his colleague. When Oftedal submitted his resignation as professor at Augsburg in 1902, Sverdrup, recalling Oftedal's vital service to the school, spoke of it as a "testing of a unique kind." Though different in personality, the two men supported and complemented each other. Sverdrup was much more the thinker, writer, and scholar. Oftedal, the activist, could and did fight battles and champion causes. Their combined impact and influence was made greater by their friendship and mutually beneficial work together.[12]

Administrative duties, teaching, writing, speaking, a rather extensive correspondence, and the strain of the controversies in which he was sometimes involved did not allow Sverdrup much time for relaxation or recreation. Yet he recognized the value of such activities and tried to take advantage of them. A good example is the Saga Hill summer colony established on Lake Minnetonka about twenty-five miles west of Minneapolis. It was started in the 1880s by a "group of professors, ministers, bankers, and professional men" who were very interested in Augsburg Seminary. The Sverdrups were not part of the original colony, but as it expanded they joined the group. Initially they rented a cottage, but later they bought lots and built a summer home in which they "planned to live the year round after his retirement." The group built a meetinghouse near the lakeshore, where they held worship services and Sunday school during the summer. Even this relaxed activity was affected by the controversies of the 1890s, since some members of the colony supported one faction and some the other. Those who joined the Lutheran Free Church bought another large house from which they created a summer home for the nurses in the Minneapolis deaconess residence. It was also used for church services and group singing. Sverdrup was among those who preached at these gatherings.[13]

He also conceived a plan for building a summer hotel as a retreat for pastors and their wives, suggesting the vicinity of Aitkin, Minnesota. In 1895 he sent a letter to pastors to discuss "how we could get a good refreshing summer hotel" at a lake, "preferably in a deep woods, where water and air and surroundings" would be "completely different from the hard prairies." He mentioned the possibilities of rest, sailing, fishing, swimming, and riding. His proposal called for the formation of a joint stock company that would issue 200 stocks at $50.00 each. Interested persons could then buy shares. The plan did not materialize as he envisioned it, but it shows his interest in that type of activity and in the kind of landscape he had known in Norway.[14]

The earlier-mentioned exchange of letters between Sverdrup and his son indicates that during the latter part of Georg's life the summer home on Lake Minnetonka offered a welcome relief from his many duties. He looked forward to going there so that he could relax, and at times he expressed the hope that the change in setting would be good for his wife's health. A note of weariness crept into some of his correspondence in later years. In 1901 he wrote to his son about reading Plato's *Phaedo* in Greek and wishing that Augsburg's students would be able to do so. Unfortunately, they were too old when they began their studies at the school, and thus were not able to attain that level of proficiency. Sverdrup saw this as an example of "the lot of the pioneer" (*nybyggerlivets kaar*) and felt "we must all share it." Still, he said, he had gone into this work with his eyes open and it had not been a disappointment. In a letter written in 1905 he told George that he hoped for a lightening of his work load when Andreas Helland joined the faculty. He wanted to do some writing "before I become too old." On April 1, 1907, slightly over a month before his death, he wrote to his son that he wanted to be relieved of the duties of the presidency so that he could devote himself to teaching. In a letter to a pastor friend in 1906 he had spoken of Augsburg as "a hard place for me, where life seems like a constant suffering." He also wrote that "perhaps God will give me some days to live in peace after I am through with my work here, so that some of the bitter taste of life here below can disappear before I die." It seems clear that the many struggles in America had taken their toll, and he looked forward to a time at the end of life when he would be able to live near the lake, freed from the onerous responsibilities of his Augsburg position.[15]

This very natural desire for a rest after the labors of life was not to be realized. Sverdrup died on May 3, 1907, near the end of another school year. He was then fifty-eight years old. He had appeared weak and tired and had complained of feeling ill for several days, yet he carried on many of his duties and made preparations for commencement. He was not able to be on campus the last two days of his life and missed the graduation exercises, but the fact that he could be up and had appeared on the veranda at home led people to think that the illness would pass. Then came the shattering news of his death, said to be caused by "paralysis of the heart." Funeral services were conducted at Augsburg Seminary and at Trinity Lutheran Church in Minneapolis. Oftedal preached, offering a moving tribute to his friend of many years in words that made a deep impression on many of those who heard them.[16] Sverdrup was buried in Lakewood Cemetery in Minneapolis.

Sverdrup's death was a great blow to Augsburg and to the Lutheran Free Church. Their most noted theologian and leader was gone. The generation that followed him attempted to be faithful to his teachings, and his influence on school and church continues to be felt.

Ten

Georg Sverdrup: An Assessment

"[T]he greatest Lutheran theologian that America has ever had." Those words were applied to Sverdrup by John O. Evjen in an essay published in 1930.[1] Students of such noted nineteenth-century American Lutheran figures as S. S. Schmucker, C. F. W. Walther, or Charles Porterfield Krauth will, no doubt, be quick to offer their demurrers. Evjen's claim is quite obviously a debatable one, but it should not be dismissed as simply the utterance of an uncritical disciple. To be sure, Evjen spent seven years at Augsburg College and Seminary in the 1890s, during which time he had ample opportunity to become familiar with and be influenced by Sverdrup's perspective. However, he also undertook a four-year period of study in Europe, earned a doctorate degree from the University of Leipzig, and went on to become a theologian of some distinction in his own right. In his writings he made clear his differences with Sverdrup's views, especially those on polity. Evjen's articles contain many helpful insights and deserve careful consideration—even when one may not agree fully with the assessment quoted in the opening sentence of this chapter.[2]

How does one take the measure of a man such as Georg Sverdrup? That of course depends in large part on the historical perspective from which one views him. If, for example, the focus is on economics or politics, one will find little in his writings that is relevant or instructive. Sverdrup must be regarded as a person for whom religious concerns were central. He needs to be seen in the context of late nineteenth- and early twentieth-century America, especially developments taking place among Norwegian Lutheran immigrants in the Midwest. His labors and writings constitute one facet of the story of Protestantism—or more specifically of Lutheranism—in America.

The thesis put forward by the historian A. M. Schlesinger, Sr., might serve as one starting point in an attempt to assess Sverdrup and his influence. As previously noted, Schlesinger maintained that during the last quarter of the nineteenth century organized religion in America faced two great challenges: "the one to its system of thought, the other to its social program." The first challenge involved primarily the many attempts to understand and deal with the implications of the theory of evolution. Much of the theological ferment of the late nineteenth and early twentieth centuries grew out of the varied reactions to the implications of Charles Darwin's *Origin of Species*, published in 1859.[3]

The second challenge was related to the growth of big industry and of cities in the post-Civil War years. Captains of industry amassed huge fortunes, while the laborers in the factories often worked long hours at low wages. Millions of the immigrants who came to America during those years contributed to these processes of industrialization and urbanization. Some religious leaders were among those who sought to justify these developments as being in accord with God's will and with societal laws, but others were profoundly disturbed that religious sanction was given to such changes. The latter expressed concern for a different type of justice and articulated a social gospel that challenged the old outlook. There was ferment in a number of the mainline Protestant denominations as these perspectives clashed with one another.

184

Assuming validity in Schlesinger's thesis, one can go on to ask: does it apply to nineteenth-century Lutherans in America? More specifically, does it apply to Norwegian Lutheran immigrants and is it useful in making an assessment of a figure such as Georg Sverdrup?

The answers are both yes and no. In general, Lutherans in this country during that period were not agitated as much as some other denominations by the kinds of intellectual and ethical questions noted above. The linguistic barriers that existed for many of them, the ascendancy of a more orthodox and conservative theological outlook in most of the Lutheran groups, and the tendency of many immigrants to find their identity in a new land by clinging to homeland customs and traditions, served as a buffer to the kind of ferment experienced by some mainline American denominations. Nevertheless, Lutherans were not immune to such forces. Some Norwegian immigrants, for example, were aware of similar ideas stimulating discussion in Norway at the time.[4]

More fruitful for the purposes of this assessment is the comment by historian Robert Michaelsen. As noted earlier, he made the point that the immigrant minister "faced the task of maintaining sufficient contact with the old ways so as to preserve the roots of faith while also adapting his ministry to the new environment." That suggests the necessity of identifying with and articulating those patterns and perspectives from which immigrant peoples would derive identity and self-respect, but doing so in a context that was considerably different from that of the Old Country. It was a task that called for considerable resourcefulness and discernment.[5]

Georg Sverdrup, while not a minister in the traditional sense of serving as a clergyman in congregations, clearly strove to be a leader among Norwegian immigrants. He sought to shape and give direction to the religious patterns and perspectives of that group. His efforts and insights won many to his views, but they

185

Sverdrup-Oftedal Memorial Hall at Augsburg, built in the 1930s:
a monument to early leaders
(Courtesy Augsburg College Archives)

also evoked considerable resistance, as indicated by the controversies that have been discussed in earlier chapters. Why these varied responses? One likely answer is suggested by linking Michaelsen's comment about the task of the immigrant minister with an observation made by N. N. Rønning. It was his contention that "Other churchmen came from Norway to preach, to teach and to work along time-honored lines. Sverdrup came to blaze new trails."[6] The responses to a trail-blazer are often varied; they might be expected to be even more so among immigrant groups—people whose understanding of themselves was changing as they adapted to a new land.

The "new trails" Sverdrup tried to blaze would lead to the restoration of what he regarded as the emancipated and vital congregation to its proper place in Lutheranism. In working for

186

that objective he functioned as an educator, a theologian, and a churchman. Some comments on those three roles will be useful in the attempt to evaluate his contributions and influence.

Sverdrup spent all of his years in America as an educator at Augsburg Seminary in Minneapolis. What was his impact in that role? Among Norwegian immigrants it seems to have been substantial, especially in the period preceding the disputes and controversies of the 1890s. Had his writings been in English, they would certainly have had a greater impact on the dominant American society. Yet even though he wrote in Norwegian, awareness of his role was not limited to that ethnic group. At the time of his death an English-language newspaper in Minneapolis spoke of him as "the greatest Norwegian Lutheran educator in the state and one of the greatest in the country."[7]

His basic concern was theological education, and he had a clear idea of what such education should be. He was convinced that it needed to break with the classics-centered program of the past so as to develop a Scriptural-historical "congregation-centered" (*menighedsmæssig*) pattern. Only in that way would a genuinely free-churchly type of pastor be produced, one who could serve the needs of a free people in a democracy.

An earlier chapter suggested that some elements of the Augsburg Plan were not so unique as Sverdrup and his colleagues might have thought. By the late nineteenth century the movement away from the classics was well under way in American theological education.[8] Something that was unique—among Norwegian immigrants at least—was that Sverdrup's philosophy of education had roots in his understanding of the congregation and the ministry. He believed that theological education fulfilled its calling only when it was in harmony with the central developments of an era. Sverdrup was convinced that the providence of God had made his historical period the opportunity for restoring the congregation. The vigor with which he expressed these views in his writings caused many Norwegian immigrants to think seriously about the nature of theological education and of higher education in general. He was also a major force in shaping the course of Augsburg Seminary during the early decades of the school's existence.

Yet his impact on Augsburg was not an unmixed blessing. The school never became the center of theological learning among Norwegian Lutheran immigrants that it might have been—and Sverdrup must bear some responsibility for that. He was not able to persuade the majority of Norwegian-American Lutherans that his approach was the best one. His sharp attack in the 1890s on what he termed humanism was unconvincing to many. The resulting impasse led to a much restricted role for the seminary.

Augsburg's development as a fully-accredited liberal arts college may also have been delayed by Sverdrup's activities. The 1874 Augsburg Plan had called for the development of a college-level department of practical studies for those students who did not intend to enter the ministry. That phase of the plan was not developed. In the 1880s Sverdrup used his influence to move the school in the direction of being exclusively a divinity school— though there were students who took the college (Greek department) course without entering the ministry. Sverdrup thought of the institution as one school whose several departments were designed to foster the main objective of preparing pastors who could serve the free congregations in America without consciousness of class. The demands and opportunities of the times, he felt, called for such a commitment. Near the end of his life he sensed that the school's program would have to be strengthened so that students who went from the college to other educational institutions in America would not be at a disadvantage. By the turn of the century the Greek department program needed improvement to meet the standards of that time. A commitment in the 1870s and 1880s to the establishment of the practical department might have aided that process. It was, however, the task of later generations at the school to correlate the Sverdrup legacy with the needs of a new situation.[9]

Georg Sverdrup was also a theologian of considerable stature. He entered vigorously into the disputes among his countrymen in America, gaining both supporters and opponents. Recent interpreters of his tradition have spoken of him as a "prophetic and creative" thinker who raised issues still on the agenda of American Lutheranism, one who might have helped to steer the course of theology among Norwegian Americans into more fruitful channels had he not become identified with a minority stance in the debates of the 1890s.[10]

Sverdrup's theological approach combined the emphasis on Christian experience derived from the famous German theologian Friedrich Schleiermacher (1768–1834), with a Lutheran confessional stance. It called for a revised understanding of the role of Scripture and a different starting point in the development of a theological system. In methodology and approach, if not always in specific doctrines, it differed from the scholasticism of seventeenth-century Lutheran orthodoxy.[11]

Sverdrup's rejection of what he called theses Christianity and his approach to Scripture indicated that he had been influenced by the nineteenth-century Erlangen theology. It was a perspective he found congenial with his pietistic heritage, stressing a vital Christianity in which the essentials of the faith were presented in a simple and straightforward manner. The special mark of his theology was his understanding of the "free and living" congregation that he felt was portrayed in the New Testament. Many of his writings were devoted to exploring the ramifications of that insight. Polity as such was not his major concern, but the congregationalism that he espoused in his later years grew out of his desire to restore what he saw as the New Testament pattern.

Sverdrup's theology, like that of his teacher Gisle Johnson in Norway, had a strong practical emphasis. It was designed to be of service to the church. One interpreter of Johnson has indicated that Johnson's lectures did not encourage independent scholarly work in systematic theology on the part of students. John Evjen said the same of Sverdrup,[12] who did not define his role as encouraging "scholarship for the sake of scholarship." Theology was to be the servant of the church. His prime concern was not to investigate the critical questions in Old Testament studies or to devise a totally new theological system. Sverdrup felt that the theologian who was truly responsible to the congregation would devote his energies to more basic tasks.

How adequate was that theological outlook to meet the challenge of some of the new ideas of the time—the challenge to "organized religion's system of thought," of which Schlesinger spoke? Could it respond meaningfully to those who felt the influence of naturalism, positivism, or evolutionary thought? It has been suggested, for example, that the new intellectual atmosphere in Norway during the late nineteenth century created a situation in which events in a sense "passed by" the Gisle Johnson outlook shared by Sverdrup, since that perspective lacked the "Christian humanistic tradition" that might have enabled it to deal more effectively with the new patterns of thought.[13]

Can the same be said of Sverdrup, one of the products of the Johnsonian tradition, in the American context? There too traditional theological systems and social programs were being challenged, and some Norwegian immigrants were becoming aware of the new ways of thinking. It seems fair to say that Sverdrup's "anti-humanistic" stance and some of the pietistic elements in his background might not have provided the best base from which to confront some of the new cultural challenges. A fear of unbelief and free-thinking marked some of his later writings. He wrote some things that buttressed the position of anti-intellectual elements among Norwegian Lutherans. For example, those Norwegian immigrants and their descendants whose piety inclined them to despise culture and learning could seemingly claim the support of Sverdrup, as evidenced in his attacks on what he termed humanism. These attacks, of course, were made on the basis of considerable learning; those who appealed to them might not have had that same background.

But certainly this much can be said for Sverdrup's stance: he was aware of some of the new patterns of thought as they affected Norwegian immigrants. Further, he was convinced that the best way to meet them was in the restoration of the free congregation in a free church in which all of the gifts of grace would be utilized to the fullest. A church free to be the church was his answer to the challenge of modern thought.

His emphasis on freedom also affirmed elements that were central to the American democratic tradition. He held that Christianity and genuine freedom were not antithetical, since true freedom was ultimately rooted in the liberating message of Christianity. At that point his stance differed markedly from some of the conservative defenders of Christianity in Norway, who sought to protect the traditional Christian viewpoint by linking it with a very conservative political outlook. Sverdrup rejected that linkage. He embraced the principle of a free church in a free state and regarded America as the place where it could best be realized. He saw the American pattern of political and religious freedom as offering precisely the setting in which the Christian community could thrive and grow. Sverdrup's theological outlook, it can be said, provided Norwegian immigrants with the model of a positive response to certain key elements in the American democratic tradition.

As noted, Sverdrup was a theologian who sought to serve the church. As a churchman he labored to lay the foundations among a group of people involved in the transition from a state church to a free church. He wanted those foundations built on genuinely free-churchly principles. He also saw no basic conflict between popular (*folkelig*) and ecclesiastical concerns. He encouraged those things that he felt would enable people to express their Christian convictions as free citizens in a new land. The outstanding example of that was his vigorous defense of the American

191

common school, in which he encouraged Norwegian immigrants to send their children to that democratic institution rather than to start their own separate congregational schools. His efforts on behalf of missions, church union, deaconess work, and lay activities also illustrate his dedication to the task of serving the needs of an immigrant people.

The controversy of the 1890s limited the scope of his activity and influence. It seems to have made him less open to some of his brethren as he saw his stance become a minority position within his church body. His principles were articulated with greater clarity, but he also seemed to be less flexible, less willing to compromise for the sake of worthy objectives. There was surely an element of tragedy in that development. Sverdrup had much to contribute, but his unbending commitment to principles, when pushed too far, could obstruct the achievement of the very goals for which he labored.

Nevertheless, Sverdrup cannot be denied the recognition that comes from striving earnestly for the causes to which he was committed. He gave of himself unstintingly. A man of scholarly background and keen mind, he chose to spend his life among people who were just establishing themselves in the New World. For almost thirty-three years his was a leading voice among them. His strong emphasis on what his mother called "living Christianity" helped to perpetuate that outlook among many Americans of Norwegian background.

This assessment of Georg Sverdrup has pointed to his vision of reviving—"restoring from the ruins"—the Christian congregation as his central concern in America. That vision, along with his convictions concerning the proper means to realize it, dominated his thinking and activities. Acceptance or rejection of that vision by his fellow Norwegian immigrants clearly determined the success or failure of his life's work.

The foundation of that vision is found in the philosophy of history that Sverdrup subscribed to, one that imparted true zeal to his activities. The best analogy that comes to mind is that of the seventeenth-century Puritans who came to these shores. Colonial historian Perry Miller has ably delineated the outlook of these immigrants on an "errand into the wilderness": he points to their view that God had "sifted the nation" in order to plant his "choice grain" in the New World; he notes their conviction that they were to execute a flank attack on the forces of evil, to become "a city set on a hill," a model of a godly society so that the rest of the world could see what a people covenanted to God could become. It was an outlook that gave drive and determination to the early Puritan settlers.[14]

Sverdrup himself once compared the Norwegian immigrants to the early Puritans. He spoke of the Puritans leaving Europe in search of religious freedom and of the fact that, after a certain amount of groping, they established full religious liberty without yielding to religious indifference. He went on to say that in this respect there was "a great similarity between the earliest and best English immigrants to America and the best Norwegian immigrants to this land. . . . Norwegians in America rejoice that they have found release from the compulsion and immaturity of the state church. At the same time it is also a joy for them to be able to participate in establishing and securing a Norwegian free church in this country." He felt the Norwegians were like the Puritans in that they had not lost their zeal for the Christian faith even though they rejoiced at being free of the state church.[15]

Sverdrup was convinced that the Norwegian people in America had also received a calling from God. He believed that God had produced the revivals of nineteenth-century Norway, and that God had led them to America, a land where religious liberty and the separation of church and state meant an opportunity to rebuild God's congregation in a way that would be pleasing to Him. A working model of a free and living congregation would then be available to Christians back in Norway. It is here, in "our free land," he once wrote, that "Norway's spiritual life shall bear its mature fruit in a free congregation."[16]

Taken on their own terms, these ideas are staggering in their implications. They involve nothing less than the idea of a new beginning in the New World under the providence of God, and the vision of creating a pattern that would be emulated by people in other countries. They gave to Sverdrup's efforts a sense of exhilaration and destiny as he labored with the belief that he was helping to achieve one of God's grand designs. Sverdrup's views become all the more remarkable when one recalls Ingrid Semmingsen's observation that a very high percentage of the Norwegian immigrants were of "the simple class"—the "People." Sverdrup saw these people as the recipients of a great calling; he regarded them as chosen instruments to further God's cause.[17]

Halvdan Koht described the Norwegian politician Johan Sverdrup, Georg's uncle, as a person of tenacious strength of will and unbreakable courage, one who was not broken by defeat. The reason, said Koht, was that "he was always convinced that he was in league with the future."[18] That same conviction permeated Georg Sverdrup's outlook. He *knew* that this was the "Age of the congregation." The opportunity that was presented must be grasped. Regardless of some failures, he would allow nothing to stand in the way.

Notes

Introduction

[1] Sverdrup's writings were collected, edited, and published in six volumes after his death by Andreas Helland under the title *Professor Georg Sverdrups samlede skrifter i udvalg* (Minneapolis, 1909–1912). They will be cited hereafter as Sverdrup, *Samlede skrifter*. See vol. 3:92 for this statement. Selections from Sverdrup's writings have been translated into English by Melvin A. Helland and published in *The Heritage of Faith: Selections from the Writings of Georg Sverdrup* (Minneapolis, 1969).

[2] Sverdrup's prominent role among Norwegian Lutherans in America is documented in such works as E. Clifford Nelson and Eugene L. Fevold, *The Lutheran Church Among Norwegian-Americans*, 2 vols. (Minneapolis, 1960); Eugene L. Fevold, *The Lutheran Free Church* (Minneapolis, 1969); and Andreas Helland, *Georg Sverdrup: The Man and His Message* (Minneapolis, 1947).

[3] John O. Evjen, "Georg Sverdrup," in Albert Hauck, ed., *Real-Encyclopadie für protestantische Theologie und Kirche*, 24 (Leipzig, 1913), 545.

Chapter One

[1] Einar Molland, *Church Life in Norway, 1800–1950*, trans. Harris Kaasa (Minneapolis, 1957), 1.

[2] Here and below, see Karen Larsen, *A History of Norway* (Princeton, New Jersey, 1948), 386. See also Andreas Seierstad, *Kyrkjelegt reformarbeid i Norig i nittande hundreaaret* (Bergen, 1923), 34-41.

[3] Larsen, *History of Norway*, 436. See pages 423-453 for her discussion of this topic.

[4] Nelson and Fevold, *Lutheran Church Among Norwegian-Americans*, 1:8. This is the definitive work on religious developments among Norwegian Lutherans in America.

[5] Francis Sejerstad, *Den vanskelige frihet 1814–1851*, vol. 10 of *Norges*

Historie, ed. by Knut Mykland (Oslo, 1978), 413-418; Larsen, *History of Norway*, 430.

[6] Works containing useful statistical information on Norwegian immigrants in America include Carlton C. Qualey, *Norwegian Settlement in the United States* (Northfield, Minnesota, 1938), and O. M. Norlie, *History of the Norwegian People in America* (Minneapolis, 1925).

[7] Ingrid Semmingsen, *Veien mot vest. Utvandringen fra Norge til Amerika 1865–1915* (Oslo, 1950), 2:50, 186, 192.

[8] A helpful discussion of these religious movements is included in Andreas Aarflot, *Norsk kirkehistorie* (Oslo, 1967), vol. 2.

[9] Walter F. Dodd, *Modern Constitutions*, 2 (Chicago, 1909), 123–125.

[10] Einar Molland, "Endringer i det religiøse liv," in Johan T. Ruud *et al.*, eds., *Dette er Norge 1814–1964* (Oslo, 1963), 1:475–502.

[11] Aarflot, *Norsk kirkehistorie*, 2:290. See also Seierstad, *Kyrkjelegt reformarbeid*, 31–60.

[12] Here and below, see Ivar Welle, *Norges kirkehistorie*, vol. 3 of *Kirkens historie* (Oslo, 1948), 191, and Martin Ski, Per Voksø, and Egil Aarvik, eds., *Kristenlivet i Norge* (Oslo, 1962), 36.

[13] Nelson and Fevold, *Lutheran Church Among Norwegian-Americans*, 1:17, 21; Molland, *Church Life in Norway*, 3–20, and "Endringer i det religiøse liv," 1:483; Joseph M. Shaw, *Pulpit Under the Sky* (Minneapolis, 1955).

[14] There are references to Hauge and the Haugean movement scattered throughout Sverdrup's writings. An example of a somewhat extended discussion is a treatise with a selection entitled "Vækkelsen ved Hauge" in his *Samlede skrifter*, 1:168–171.

[15] J. C. Heuch, "Gisle Johnson," in Gerhard Gran, ed., *Nordmænd i det 19de aarhundrede* (Kristiania, 1914), 2:71; Molland, *Church Life in Norway*, 35.

[16] See Godvin Ousland, *En kirkehøvding. Professor Gisle Johnson som teolog og kirkemann* (Oslo, 1950), for a helpful discussion of Johnson's life and thought. A brief summary of the portion of that book dealing with the German and Danish influences on Johnson is given in James S. Hamre, "A Norwegian Influence: Gisle Johnson," in *Luther Theological Seminary Review*, 10 (November, 1971), 18–25.

[17] Nelson and Fevold, *Lutheran Church Among Norwegian-Americans*, 1:34.

[18] See Sverdrup, *Samlede skrifter*, 1:193–197, 209–211.

[19] Seierstad, *Kyrkjelegt reformarbeid*, 63.

[20] Aarflot, *Norsk kirkehistorie*, 2:292.

[21] Nelson and Fevold, *Lutheran Church Among Norwegian-Americans*, 1:38.

[22] See Aarflot, *Norsk kirkehistorie*, 2:418–422.

[23] Sverdrup, *Samlede skrifter*, 1:202.

[24] See the first issue of *Ny Luthersk Kirketidende* (1877), 3, a periodical edited by Jakob Sverdrup and O. Vollan, which expressed the views of the friends of church reform.

[25] Here and below, see Ivar Welle, *Kirkens historie*, 2:152 (Oslo, 1951).

[26] Halvdan Koht, *Johan Sverdrup*, 3 vols. (Kristiania, 1918, 1922, 1925), 1:14.

[27] Peder Michelsen's wife's name is not known. Genealogical informa-

tion on the Sverdrup family is available in such works as Martin Arnesen and J. Sverdrup, *Stamtavle over slægten Sverdrup* (Kristiania, 1885); S. H. Finne-Grønn, *Slegten Sverdrup. Kortfattede genealogisk-personalhistoriske oplysninger med prospekter og portrætter* (Christiania, 1923); Ragnhild Sverdrup, "Slegten Sverdrup. Kortfattede oplysninger om Harald Ulrik Sverdrups (sen.) efterslegt" (1969), in Universitetsbiblioteket, Oslo. The first chapter of Helland's *Georg Sverdrup: The Man and His Message* contains a discussion of the Sverdrup family in Norwegian life and history, with special reference to the line leading to Georg.

[28] Larsen, *History of Norway*, 377–383; Einar Boyesen, *Hartvig Nissen 1815-1874 og det norske skolevesens reform*, 2 vols. (Oslo, 1947), 1:30.

[29] Finne-Grønn, *Slegten Sverdrup*, 63.

[30] Koht, *Johan Sverdrup*, 1:3.

[31] Finne-Grønn, *Slegten Sverdrup*, 78–80; *Norsk biografisk leksikon*, 15 (Oslo, 1966), 438-444; Helland, *Georg Sverdrup*, 14–18.

[32] *Norsk biografisk leksikon*, 15:395–403; Christopher Bruun and Thv. Klaveness, eds., *For Kirke og Kultur*, 6 (Kristiania, 1899), 321–324; Helland, *Georg Sverdrup*, 20.

Chapter Two

[1] Carl H. Chrislock, *From Fjord to Freeway: 100 Years — Augsburg College* (Minneapolis, 1969), 62.

[2] Karl Schiørn, *Familien Schiørn. Genealogisk-personal-historiske oplysninger* (Tønsberg, 1935), 18. Schiørn's support of the cause of church reform can be seen in an essay entitled "Om Konfirmationstvangen," published in Gisle Johnson, ed., *Luthersk Kirketidende* (Christiania, 1870), 417–426. The essay is a stinging denunciation of a law requiring confirmation: Schiørn argues that coerced confirmation is an abomination, is contrary to the nature of faith, and conflicts with Christ's way of doing things.

[3] John O. Evjen, "Georg Sverdrup," in Lars Lillehei, ed., *Augsburg Seminary and the Lutheran Free Church* (Minneapolis, 1928), 6.

[4] A. Holmesland et al., eds., *Aschehougs konversasjonsleksikon*, 14 (Oslo, 1971), 616.

[5] See Otto Anderssen, *Realisme eller klassicisme. Et kapitel av 1830 aarenes kulturkamp* (Kristiania, 1921).

[6] Here and below, see Boyesen, *Hartvig Nissen*, 1:57–72, and Ernst J. Borup and Frederik Schrøder, comps., *Haandbog i N.F.S. Grundtvigs skrifter*, (København, 1929), vol. 1. The first volume of this collection is entitled *Grundtvigs skoletanker*.

[7] Boyesen, *Hartvig Nissen*, 1:77–83.

[8] "Det kongl. norske Frederiks universitets matricul for aaret 1865," in *Norske universitets- og skole-annaler*, 6, Universitetets Secretair, Tredie Række (Christiania, 1866), 318.

[9] See "Affidavit," in Lillehei, *Augsburg Seminary*, 133.

[10] See John O. Evjen's articles entitled "Georg Sverdrup," in Lillehei, *Augsburg Seminary*, 6, and in Hauck, *Real-Encyclopadie für protestantische Theologie*, 24:538. Evjen indicates that the University of Erlangen list of

students matriculated for the years 1866–1873 did not include the name of Georg Sverdrup.

[11] Gerhard Gran, ed., *Det kongelige Frederiks universitet 1811–1911. Festskrift* (Kristiania, 1911), 1:279.

[12] Fredrik B. Wallem, *Det norske studentersamfund gjennem hundrede aar 1813 – 2. oktober 1913*, 1 (Kristiania, 1916), 530–572.

[13] "Det kongl. norske Frederiks universitets matricul for aaret 1866," 18.

[14] Andreas Brandrud, "Teologien," in Gran, *Det kongelige Frederiks universitet. Festskrift*, 1:3–62. The other members of the theological faculty were Rasmus T. Nissen (church history) and J. F. Dietrichson (New Testament). In 1869 student of theology Fredrick Peterson began giving lectures, among them a series on the literary activity of Søren Kierkegaard.

[15] These may be found in the Augsburg College Archives.

[16] J. Sverdrup, G. Sverdrup, and G. Schielderup, eds., *Kirkelige traktater* (Kristiania, 1869–1870). Three of the tracts were written by Schielderup and one each by the Sverdrup brothers. The one by Georg Sverdrup, entitled "Om konfirmationenes frigivelse," may be found in his *Samlede skrifter*, 2:331–338.

[17] Georg Sverdrup's *eksamensbesvarelser* have been preserved in the Norsk Historisk Kjeldeskrift-Institutt in Oslo.

[18] Here and two paragraphs below, see Sverdrup's paper, "Kirkens forhold til staten," a lengthy discussion of the topic in the *eksamensbevarelser*.

[19] "Det kongl. norske Frederiks universitets matricul for aaret 1871," 32; "Affidavit," in Lillehei, *Augsburg Seminary*, 133.

[20] "Indberetning om et studieophold i Paris i 1873," in *Norske universitets - og skole-annaler*, 12:225–231.

[21] See "Menigheden i katakomberne," in Sverdrup's *Samlede skrifter*, 1:147–166; Helland, *Georg Sverdrup*, 212. For the English sermon, see Sverdrup, *Samlede skrifter*, 6:315–323.

[22] J. A. Bergh, *Den norsk lutherske kirkes historie i Amerika* (Minneapolis, 1914), 242; Helland, *Georg Sverdrup*, 236; Evjen, "Georg Sverdrup," in Lillehei, *Augsburg Seminary*, 7.

Chapter Three

[1] Sverdrup, *Samlede skrifter*, 3:91; Helland, *Georg Sverdrup*, 46.

[2] Henry F. Bedford and Trevor Colbourn, *The Americans: A Brief History* (New York, 1972), 245, 247.

[3] Qualey, *Norwegian Settlement*, 4; Norlie, *History of the Norwegian People in America*, 72–74, 231.

[4] Bergh, *Den norsk lutherske kirkes historie i Amerika*, 525.

[5] For a more detailed discussion of these and subsequent developments among the Norwegian Lutheran groups discussed here and two paragraphs below, see Nelson and Fevold, *Lutheran Church Among Norwegian-Americans*.

[6] Sverdrup, *Samlede skrifter*, 1:223; 3:91.

[7] Histories of the school include Andreas Helland, *Augsburg Seminar gjennem femti aar, 1869–1919* (Minneapolis, 1920), and Chrislock, *From Fjord*

to Freeway. Noting that there has been some debate over which school should be called "the first (or oldest) Norwegian seminary in America," Helland offers arguments claiming this distinction for Augsburg.

[8] Weenaas (1835–1924) was born and educated in Norway and served as a pastor there for several years before coming to America in 1868. He was president and professor at Augsburg Seminary from 1869 to 1876. He returned to Norway in 1876 but came back to America again from 1882 to 1885 as a theological professor at Red Wing Seminary in Red Wing, Minnesota. He then went back to Norway, where he engaged in pastoral work. See Helland, *Augsburg Seminar*, 55, 361.

[9] Helland, *Augsburg Seminar*, 363; Evjen, "Georg Sverdrup," in Hauck, *Real-Encyclopadie*, 24:538.

[10] Gunnersen (1844–1904) was born and educated in Norway. He was a professor at Augsburg Seminary from 1874 to 1883, served a year at Red Wing Seminary, and returned to Norway in 1884, where he was a pastor until his death. See Helland, *Augsburg Seminar*, 363, and Bergh, *Den norsk lutherske kirkes historie i Amerika*, 241.

[11] "Han var *fornuften*, mens Gunnersen var *hjertet* og Oftedal var *aanden*, i det nye triumvirat." Here and below, see August Weenaas, *Livserindringer fra Norge og Amerika* (Bergen, 1935), 158; *Mindeblade eller otte aar i Amerika* (Volda, 1890).

[12] Here and two paragraphs below, see *Beretning af Konferentsen*, 1874, 59–64; Helland, *Augsburg Seminar*, 347–351. A helpful discussion of these developments is included in Chrislock, *From Fjord to Freeway*, 20–23.

[13] "Program for Augsburg Seminarium med collegeavdelinger, vedtat i direktionsmøte 31te aug. 1874, tillikemed forklarende bemerkninger av fakultetet" is included in Helland, *Augsburg Seminar*, 442–452. The author has adopted Chrislock's rendering of this title into English; see *From Fjord to Freeway*, 20. In another of his writings, Andreas Helland comments: "Just by whom the 'Remarks' which form the largest and in some ways most important part of the *Program* were drafted, it is impossible to determine with absolute certainty, but it is more than likely that Sverdrup was the author. That all the three younger men had discussed the ideas which are contained in them is quite certain." See Helland, *Georg Sverdrup*, 49. Sverdrup himself indicated that he was the author of the comments on the Greek department. See "Affidavit," in Lillehei, *Augsburg Seminary*, 133–141.

[14] Here and two paragraphs below, see Helland, *Augsburg Seminar*, 442.

[15] Jakob Sverdrup, "Augsburg Seminarium bedømt i Norge," in *Kvartal-Skrift*, 1875, 82–90.

[16] *Beretning af Konferentsen*, 1875, 64; 1876, 39.

[17] Winton U. Solberg, *The University of Illinois 1867–1894: An Intellectual and Cultural History* (Urbana, Illinois, 1968), 8.

[18] See, for example, Charles Francis Adams, *A College Fetich: An Address Delivered Before the Harvard Chapter of the Fraternity of the Phi Beta Kappa* (Boston, 1883); George P. Schmidt, *The Liberal Arts College: A Chapter in American Cultural History* (New Brunswick, New Jersey, 1957); Richard

Hofstadter and C. DeWitt Hardy, *The Development and Scope of Higher Education in the United States* (New York, 1952); John S. Brubacher and Willis Rudy, *Higher Education in Transition* (New York, 1968); and R. Freeman Butts, *The College Charts Its Course* (New York, 1939).

[19] Karen Larsen, *Laur. Larsen: Pioneer College President* (Northfield, Minnesota, 1936), 140–185.

[20] Chrislock, *From Fjord to Freeway*, 27.

[21] *Beretning af Konferentsen*, 1877, 53; Sverdrup, *Samlede skrifter*, 3:31.

[22] *Beretning af Konferentsen*, 1877, 59; 1879, 32; 1884, 40, 77.

[23] Sverdrup, *Samlede skrifter*, 3:41; *Beretning af Konferentsen*, 1885, 28; Chrislock, *From Fjord to Freeway*, 31–35, 37–39; Helland, *Georg Sverdrup*, 118.

[24] *Beretning af Konferentsen*, 1877, 55. In 1877 Norwegian immigrants had neither the material resources nor the trained teachers for such a program. Near the turn of the century, an academy movement made some headway in Norwegian-American education. Patterned after American high schools rather than Norwegian folk schools, these academies nevertheless fulfilled some of Sverdrup's objectives.

[25] "Affidavit," in Lillehei, *Augsburg Seminary*, 139.

[26] Many of these writings have been included in his *Samlede skrifter*, 3:165–212. Like other educational institutions in America, Augsburg found it difficult to escape financial concerns about its continued existence.

[27] Helland, *Augsburg Seminar*, 378.

[28] Helland, *Georg Sverdrup*, 184; Evjen, "Georg Sverdrup," in Hauck, *Real-Encyclopadie*, 24:541, 546; Sverdrup, *Samlede skrifter*, 3:4.

[29] Evjen, "Georg Sverdrup," in both Lillehei, *Augsburg Seminary*, 11, and Hauck, *Real-Encyclopadie*, 24:541. The Formula of Concord was a document accepted by many German Lutherans in 1580 to put an end to some theological disputes. It later came to be regarded as a confessional statement by Lutherans in several countries.

[30] Bergh, *Den norsk lutherske kirkes historie i Amerika*, 242.

Chapter Four

[1] Nelson and Fevold, *Lutheran Church Among Norwegian-Americans*, 1:241.

[2] Here and three paragraphs below, see J. L. Neve and O. W. Heick, *A History of Christian Thought*, 2 (Philadelphia, 1946), 131–138; Sverdrup, *Samlede skrifter*, vol. 5. Volume 5 of Sverdrup's collected writings, entitled "Indledning til Det gamle Testamente tilligemed en oversigt over nogle af de bibelske Bøger," provides insights into Sverdrup's understanding of and approach to Scripture.

[3] These lectures and the letters in the next paragraph may be found in the Augsburg College Archives.

[4] For a thorough discussion of the influence of Erlangen theology on nineteenth-century Norwegian developments, see Ousland, *En kirkehøvding*.

[5] *Aaben erklæring* is included in Helland, *Augsburg Seminar*, 440–442.

[6] Sverdrup, *Samlede skrifter*, 1:223.

[7] Sverdrup, *Samlede skrifter*, 2:2–4.

[8] Sverdrup, *Samlede skrifter*, 1:255–310.

[9] Nelson and Fevold, *Lutheran Church Among Norwegian-Americans*, 1:242.

[10] Sverdrup, *Samlede skrifter*, 1:234–278. Erik Pontoppidan (1698–1764) was a Lutheran bishop whose *Sandhed til gudfrygtighed* was a widely used explanation of Luther's Small Catechism; see Nelson and Fevold, *Lutheran Church Among Norwegian-Americans*, 1:10.

[11] Sverdrup, *Samlede skrifter*, 4:188.

[12] Sverdrup, *Samlede skrifter*, 1:255–278.

[13] Sverdrup, *Samlede skrifter*, 1:292–310.

[14] Nelson and Fevold, *Lutheran Church Among Norwegian-Americans*, 1:254; see 253–270 for a discussion of this controversy.

[15] Sverdrup, *Samlede skrifter*, 4:71–83. See also the manuscript entitled "Naade, Frihed og Nødvendighed," Augsburg College Archives.

[16] Discussions of the course of this controversy and the issues involved are included in Theodore C. Blegen, *Norwegian Migration to America*, 2 (Northfield, Minnesota, 1940), 241–276; Laurence M. Larson, *The Changing West and Other Essays* (Northfield, Minnesota, 1937), 116–146; Frank C. Nelsen, "The School Controversy Among Norwegian Immigrants," in *Norwegian-American Studies*, 26 (Northfield, Minnesota, 1974), 206–219; and James S. Hamre, "Norwegian Immigrants Respond to the 'Common' School: A Case Study of American Values and the Lutheran Tradition," in *Church History*, 50 (1981), 302–315.

[17] Here and below, see "Commonskolen," in Sverdrup, *Samlede skrifter*, 1:358–384. Portions of this essay have been translated into English in Helland, *The Heritage of Faith*, 87–99. A more complete translation is included in James S. Hamre, "Georg Sverdrup's Concept of the Role and Calling of the Norwegian-American Lutherans: An Annotated Translation of Selected Writings" (Ph.D. dissertation, University of Iowa, 1967), 100–135; Blegen, *Norwegian Migration to America*, 2:270.

[18] In his *The Winning of the Midwest: Social and Political Conflict, 1888–1896* (Chicago, 1971), Richard Jensen divides Midwestern religious groups into pietists and liturgicals. He sees the two outlooks as expressing differing attitudes on a number of issues, such as prohibition, Sunday laws, and public and parochial schools. See especially chapter 3, "Pietists and Liturgicals: The Religious Roots of Partisanship."

[19] Sverdrup, *Samlede skrifter*, 4:263.

[20] Sverdrup, *Samlede skrifter*, 4:188.

[21] Sverdrup, *Samlede skrifter*, 4:169–179.

[22] Sverdrup, *Samlede skrifter*, 4:180–199.

[23] Sverdrup, *Samlede skrifter*, 4:223.

[24] Sverdrup, *Samlede skrifter*, 1:70–146; 4:180–199.

[25] Molland, *Church Life in Norway*, 66–81.

[26] Sverdrup, *Samlede skrifter*, 2:101–119. See also his "Amerika og Menigheden" (America and the Congregation), in *Samlede skrifter*, 4:370–376. Hamre's annotated translation of that address is included in *Norwegian-American Studies*, 24 (Northfield, Minnesota, 1970), 137–147.

[27] *Beretning af Konferentsen*, 1876, 29,42,46,47.

[28] Bergh, *Den norsk lutherske kirkes historie i Amerika*, 244.

[29] C. L. Clausen, *Prof. Georg Sverdrups angreb og Pastorerne J. Olsens og C. L. Clausens tilsvar* (Chicago, 1881), 22.

[30] Here and below, see Sverdrup, *Samlede skrifter*, 4:243–248.

[31] Here and below, see Clausen, *Sverdrups angreb og Olsens og Clausens tilsvar*, 10–70, 73–78.

[32] Here and below, see *Beretning af Konferentsen*, 1883, 32–39; Helland, *Georg Sverdrup*, 100–111; Clausen, *Sverdrups angreb og Olsens og Clausens tilsvar*, 83–90; Nelson and Fevold, *Lutheran Church Among Norwegian-Americans*, 1:225-238; Bergh, *Den norsk lutherske kirkes historie i Amerika*, 273–282.

[33] Helland, *Georg Sverdrup*, 68; Nelson and Fevold, *Lutheran Church Among Norwegian-Americans*, 1:234.

[34] Here and two paragraphs below, see J. A. Bergh, *Den gamle og nye retning* (Chicago, 1884).

[35] Sverdrup, *Samlede skrifter*, 2:120–143. Nelson and Fevold have correctly noted that one of the differences between the two directions was the tendency of men such as Sverdrup to legitimize divisions in the church of Christ on the basis of a "calling" or task to perform. However, the comment is made in a footnote that "Sverdrup said that the New School [or new direction] was a church body, not a party. The implication was that it was divinely ordained." It seems clear to this author, on the contrary, that a careful reading of Sverdrup's article will show that he is not claiming that the new direction was a church body, but that the *Conference* was a church body rather than a party. The difference has important implications for Sverdrup's stance. See Nelson and Fevold, *Lutheran Church Among Norwegian-Americans*, 1:236n.

[36] Helland, *Georg Sverdrup*, 112.

[37] Bergh, *Den norsk lutherske kirkes historie i Amerika*, 278.

[38] Sverdrup, *Samlede skrifter*, 3:197.

[39] Nelson and Fevold, *Lutheran Church Among Norwegian-Americans*, 2:285n.

[40] Leonard J. Trinterud, *The Forming of an American Tradition* (Freeport, New York, 1949), 174.

Chapter Five

[1] The manuscript is in the Augsburg College Archives.

[2] *Beretning af Konferentsen*, 1875, 92; *Beretning af Forenede Kirke*, 1890, 44–46.

[3] Here and below, see Sverdrup's annual reports to the church body, excerpts of which are included in his *Samlede skrifter*, 3:30–89.

[4] Here and below, see *Lutheraneren og Missionsbladet*, June, 1877, 182; May, 1880, 133.

[5] Most of the August, 1879, issue was taken up with the Clausen-Sverdrup- J. Olsen exchange. Sverdrup's editorial, "Som Faar, der ikke have Hyrde," was published in the May, 1881, issue.

[6] *Beretning af Konferentsen*, 1881, 56; *Lutheraneren*, October, 1885, 289.

[7] Its full title was *Kvartal-Skrift for den norsk lutherske Kirke i Amerika*.

Andreas Helland has written that the "members of the faculty contributed 61 per cent, while 39 per cent consisted of translated articles and sketches, surveys of church news, correspondences from Norway, etc." He notes too that Sverdrup contributed 417 of the 802 pages by the Augsburg faculty. See his *Georg Sverdrup*, 52, 291n. For a more complete discussion of this quarterly, see James S. Hamre, "The 'Augsburg Triumvirate' and the *Kvartalskrift*," in *Luther Theological Seminary Review* (November, 1972), 21–30.

[8] Advertisements promoting *Kvartal-Skrift* can be found in *Lutheraneren* and *Folkebladet*.

[9] *Kvartal-Skrift*, 1875, 3–10; 1878, 10.

[10] *Folkebladet*, August, 1880.

[11] This was clearly illustrated in the comments made in connection with Bjørnstjerne Bjørnson's tour of America in the early 1880s. He was viewed as an apostle of *fritænkeri*. For a discussion of *Folkebladet's* response to the Unitarian movement among Norwegian immigrants, see Nina Draxten's *Kristofer Janson in America* (Boston, 1976), 59–62, 128.

[12] *Folkebladet*, August 10, 1882; February 8, 1883; *Beretning af Konferentsen*, 1883, 34. Andreas Helland has stated that "through correspondence and otherwise," the friendship among the three men eventually was restored; see *Georg Sverdrup*, 111.

[13] Here and below, see *Folkebladet*, January 17, 1884; *Beretning af Konferentsen*, 1883, 64.

[14] The manuscript is in the Augsburg College Archives.

[15] Here and below, see Sverdrup, *Samlede skrifter*, 4:204–225.

[16] Here and below, see Sverdrup, *Samlede skrifter*, 4:204–220.

[17] *Lutheraneren og Missionsbladet*, May, 1880, 149.

[18] Here and below, see Sverdrup, *Samlede skrifter*, 4:249–252; 3:139–141.

[19] *Lutheraneren*, June 25, 1887, 207; *Beretning af Konferentsen*, 1887, 85–88.

[20] C. K. Solberg, "Zionsforeningen for Israel," in N. C. Brun, ed., *Fra ungdomsaar* (Minneapolis, 1915), 265; an example from *Lutheraneren* is the lead article in the issue of September, 1880, in which the editor gives a positive evaluation of the society and urges people to support it.

[21] Sverdrup, *Samlede skrifter*, 4:250.

[22] For a more detailed discussion of the union efforts, see Nelson and Fevold, *Lutheran Church Among Norwegian-Americans*, 2:3–37.

[23] Here and below, see Sverdrup, *Samlede skrifter*, 4:88–105.

[24] Sverdrup, *Samlede skrifter*, 4:108, 119, 122, 138.

[25] Here and below, see Sverdrup, *Samlede skrifter*, 4:116, 134, 226.

[26] Here and below, see Sverdrup, *Samlede skrifter*, 4:95, 312; *Lutheraneren*, July, 1880, 202–204, 211–214; S. M. Krogness and Th. Eggen, eds., *Referat af forhandlingerne i en Frikonference i Holden, Minnesota* (Decorah, Iowa, 1883), 5, 62.

[27] Sverdrup, *Samlede skrifter*, 4:125–142.

[28] S. M. Krogness, ed., *Referat af forhandlingerne i andet fællesmøde... afholdt i Gol, Goodhue Co., Minn.* (Chicago, [1886]); *Lutheraneren*, July 16, 1887, 232; September 1, 1888, 280; Eugene L. Fevold, "Norwegian-American Lutheranism, 1870–1890," (Ph.D. dissertation, University of Chicago, 1951), 400.

[29] Nelson and Fevold, *Lutheran Church Among Norwegian-Americans*, 2:4–16; *Fællesmødet i Scandinavia, Wis., fra 15de til 21de nov. 1888.*

[30] *Folkebladet*, January 16, 1889; Sverdrup, *Samlede skrifter*, 4:143–145; *Lutheraneren*, June 21, 1890, 208.

[31] Bergh, *Den norsk lutherske kirkes historie i Amerika*, 241.

[32] Sidney E. Mead, *The Lively Experiment: The Shaping of Christianity in America* (New York, 1963), 14.

Chapter Six

[1] Henry Steele Commager, *The American Mind: An Interpretation of American Thought and Character Since the 1880s* (New Haven, Connecticut, 1950), 41–54.

[2] Arthur M. Schlesinger, Sr., "A Critical Period in American Protestantism, 1875–1900," in *Massachusetts Historical Society Proceedings*, LXIV (June, 1932), 523–548.

[3] The brief description in *Beretning af forenede Kirke*, 1890, 8, is one example.

[4] In 1963 the Lutheran Free Church became a part of the American Lutheran Church. At that time the seminary division at Augsburg merged its faculty with that of Luther Theological Seminary in St. Paul. Augsburg College continues as a four-year liberal arts college in Minneapolis.

[5] See *Katalog for Augsburg Seminarium* (Minneapolis, 1891), 5–10; Sverdrup, *Samlede skrifter*, 3:51.

[6] *Beretning af forenede Kirke*, 1890, 117. An English translation of the Articles of Union is included in Nelson and Fevold, *Lutheran Church Among Norwegian-Americans*, 2:338–341.

[7] *Fællesmødet for "Den forenede Kirke,"* 1890, 66–68.

[8] Here and below, see *Beretning af forenede Kirke*, 1890, 117; *Fællesmødet for "Den forenede Kirke,"* 1890. Helpful accounts of the institution are William C. Benson, *High on Manitou: A History of St. Olaf College (1874–1949)* (Northfield, Minnesota, 1949), and Joseph M. Shaw, *History of St. Olaf College, 1874–1974* (Northfield, Minnesota, 1974).

[9] The August 5, 1891, issue of *Folkebladet* reproduced the famous "A. Eriksen" letter. See the July 29 issue for a statement by Albert E. Egge.

[10] *Folkebladet*, February 18, 1891. See also the issues for February 25, March 4, 11, 18, 25, April 8, 15, 22, 29, and May 13, 27, for articles in which the exchange was carried on.

[11] *Beretning af forenede Kirke*, 1891, 91–95; Sverdrup, *Samlede skrifter*, 3:49–52.

[12] *Folkebladet*, November 18, 1891.

[13] Chrislock, *From Fjord to Freeway*, 49.

[14] Nelson and Fevold, *Lutheran Church Among Norwegian-Americans*, 2:339, 341.

[15] Here and below, see *Beretning af forenede Kirke*, 1892, 198–205,182–184; Chrislock, *From Fjord to Freeway*, 65.

[16] Here and two paragraphs below, see *Beretning af forenede Kirke*, 1892, 20–22, 62–67,122,130,145,158.

[17] Chrislock, *From Fjord to Freeway*, 69–71.

[18] *Beretning af forenede Kirke*, 1893, 23, 194–203. St Olaf was without official synodical support until 1899, when it was again accepted as a college of the United Church.

[19] Here and below, see *Beretning af forenede Kirke*, 1893, 185; *Referat fra mødet af Augsburgs Venner*, 1893, 23, 30, 33; C. Saugstad, *Augsburgs historie* (Minneapolis, 1893), 31–42.

[20] *Referat fra mødet af Augsburgs Venner*, 1893, 17.

[21] Chrislock, *From Fjord to Freeway*, 77–80.

[22] Andreas Helland has gathered these *Folkebladet* articles together under two general headings in Sverdrup's *Samlede skrifter*, 3:214–240. The first heading is "Humanismen og presteuddannelsen" and the second, "Menighedsmæssig presteuddannelse." Excerpts from these articles have been translated into English in Helland, *Heritage of Faith*, 105–112. A more extensive English translation is included in Hamre, "Georg Sverdrup's Concept of the Role and Calling of the Norwegian-American Lutherans," 137–179.

[23] Here and two paragraphs below, see Sverdrup, *Samlede skrifter*, 3:217–219, 222, 231.

[24] Here and below, see Sverdrup, *Samlede skrifter*, 3:228, 233–238.

[25] Sverdrup, *Samlede skrifter*, 3:58, 74, 239; *Catalogue of Augsburg Seminary, 1896–97*, (Minneapolis, n.d.), 3.

[26] *Catalogue of Augsburg Seminary, 1894-95*, (Minneapolis, 1895), 3; *Catalogue of Augsburg Seminary, 1899–1900*, (Minneapolis, n.d.), 3.

[27] Sverdrup, *Samlede skrifter*, 3:24–28, 72.

[28] Chrislock, *From Fjord to Freeway*, 62.

[29] *Catalogue of Augsburg Seminary, 1899–1900*, 3.

[30] Sverdrup, *Samlede skrifter*, 3:7–14, 24–28; 4:370–376.

[31] The *Folkebladet* articles are included in Sverdrup, *Samlede skrifter*, 4:332–350; the articles in *Lutheraneren* were published in 1886 under the title "Tanker paa Veien."

[32] Sverdrup, *Samlede skrifter*, 4:341–347.

[33] The letter, dated March 12, 1903, has been preserved in Universitetsbiblioteket, Oslo.

[34] Molland, *Church Life in Norway*, 87.

[35] J. C. Heuch, *Mod strømmen* (Kristiania, 1902). Heuch stated that he was "driven by the deepest indignation" to register this protest against "rationalism in its modern German forms."

[36] *The Confessions of St. Augustine*, trans. Rex Warner (New York, 1963), Book One, Chapters 13–15.

[37] Will Herberg, "Religion and Education in America," in James Ward Smith and A. Leland Jamison, eds., *Religious Perspectives in American Culture*, volume 2 of *Religion in American Life* (Princeton, New Jersey, 1961), 12–17. See also Philip Leon, *The Professors: An Inaugural Lecture Delivered at University College Leicester* (Leicester, 1955), and Douglas Sloan, *The Scottish Enlightenment and the American College Ideal* (New York, 1971).

Chapter Seven

[1] Robert Michaelsen, "The Protestant Ministry in America: 1850 to the Present," in H. R. Niebuhr and Daniel D. Williams, eds., *The Ministry in Historical Perspectives* (New York, 1956), 269.

[2] See J. L. Schaver, *The Polity of the Churches* (Chicago, 1947), 21–77, for a discussion of these patterns.

[3] Stow Persons, *American Minds: A History of Ideas* (New York, 1958), 26–33.

[4] Julius Bodensieck, ed., *The Encyclopedia of the Lutheran Church*, 1 (Minneapolis, 1965), 519–526.

[5] See such works as A. R. Wentz, *A Basic History of Lutheranism in America* (Philadelphia, 1955), and E. Clifford Nelson, ed., *The Lutherans in North America* (Philadelphia, 1975), for an indication of the role of polity issues in the various Lutheran groups that developed in America.

[6] A manuscript which Andreas Helland described as "an address which the author [Sverdrup] delivered in the Theological Society at the University of Oslo in the spring of 1869, when he was only a few months past twenty years of age" has been preserved in Sverdrup, *Samlede skrifter*, 2:39–53. See also Helland, *Georg Sverdrup*, 218.

[7] Sverdrup, *Samlede skrifter*, 2:142.

[8] Sverdrup, *Samlede skrifter*, 4:256.

[9] Evjen, "Georg Sverdrup," in Hauck, *Real-Encyclopadie*, 24:553.

[10] *Referat fra mødet af Augsburgs Venner*, 1893, 23, 29–30; Saugstad, *Augsburgs historie*, 31–42.

[11] See the sermons and reports in *Referat fra mødet af Augsburgs Venner*, 1893, and *Beretning fra mødet af Augsburgs Venner* for 1894–1896.

[12] *Referat fra mødet af Augsburgs Venner*, 1893, 40–50; *Beretning fra mødet af Augsburgs Venner*, 1894, 20, 36–53, 75, 80, 87; 1895, 16, 31–36.

[13] *Beretning af forenede Kirke*, 1895, 134; *Beretning fra mødet af Augsburgs Venner*, 1895, 20, 42; Fevold, *The Lutheran Free Church*, 79–93.

[14] Sverdrup, *Samlede skrifter*, 2:144–156.

[15] Clarence J. Carlsen, *The Years of Our Church* (Minneapolis, 1942), 32; *Beretning af Frikirken*, 1897, 13, 16, 47–50.

[16] These *Folkebladet* articles have been included in Sverdrup, *Samlede skrifter*, 3:265–293. They have been translated into English in Hamre, "Georg Sverdrup's Concept of the Role and Calling of the Norwegian-American Lutherans," 203–249.

[17] Here and below, see Sverdrup, *Samlede skrifter*, 3:265–268, 271.

[18] Evjen, "Georg Sverdrup," in Hauck, *Real-Encyclopadie*, 24:545.

[19] Sverdrup, *Samlede skrifter*, 6:xiii–xvi.

[20] Sverdrup, *Samlede skrifter*, 3:268–272, 276–280.

[21] Sverdrup, *Samlede skrifter*, 2:229–252.

[22] Sverdrup, *Samlede skrifter*, 3:279–284.

[23] Sverdrup, *Samlede skrifter*, 3:284–293, 350; Winthrop S. Hudson, *The Great Tradition of the American Churches* (New York, 1963), 19.

[24] Sverdrup, *Samlede skrifter*, 4:161–168. In a letter written in 1906 Sverd-

rup excluded the possibility of co-operation with the Norwegian Synod because "we cannot co-operate with those who are dead." Sverdrup to Pastor Berlie, February 9, 1906, in Augsburg College Archives.

[25] See Rule 6 of the "Regler for Arbeide" included in Fevold, *The Lutheran Free Church*, 304–306.

[26] Nelson, *The Lutherans in North America*, 343.

[27] Sverdrup, *Samlede skrifter*, 2:157–181. Other examples of the exchanges with the United Church may be found on pages 182–192 and 193–228 in the same volume.

[28] Examples may be found in Sverdrup, *Samlede skrifter*, 2:253–287, 321–330, 339–343, 354–381; 3:358–369; 4:281–291, 298–304.

[29] Sverdrup, *Samlede skrifter*, 3:361–364, 370–379; 2:344–353.

[30] Evjen, "Georg Sverdrup," in Hauck, *Real-Encyclopadie*, 24:545.

[31] Evjen, "Georg Sverdrup," in Hauck, *Real-Encyclopadie*, 24:545.

Chapter Eight

[1] *Beretning om Frikirkens møde*, 1897–1902.

[2] Fevold, *The Lutheran Free Church*, 113.

[3] See Sverdrup, *Samlede skrifter*, 3:24–28, 241–245, 347–353, 370–379; 4:363–369.

[4] Sverdrup, *Samlede skrifter*, 3:358–369.

[5] The manuscripts may be found in the Augsburg College Archives. The *Folkebladet* articles are the source for the next five paragraphs; they are excerpted in Sverdrup, *Samlede skrifter*, 4:305–331.

[6] Helland, *Georg Sverdrup*, 193–197; Sverdrup, *Samlede skrifter*, 4:370–376.

[7] See, for example, N. N. Rønning, *Fifty Years in America* (Minneapolis, 1938), 145.

[8] See the manuscripts of sermons and meditations in Augsburg College Archives; Sverdrup, *Samlede skrifter*, 4:351–354; 6:287–297.

[9] Sven Oftedal and Georg Sverdrup, *Aand og liv. Prædikener over alle tre tekstrækkers evangelier* (Minneapolis, 1898). See also Sverdrup, *Samlede skrifter*, 6:298–329.

[10] Ousland, *En kirkehøvding*, 95–105, 294; Sverdrup, *Samlede skrifter*, 1:200. See also Søren Kierkegaard, *The Point of View of My Work as An Author: A Report to History*, trans. Walter Lowrie (New York, 1962), 5–43; S. Kierkegaard, *Attack Upon 'Christendom'*, trans. Walter Lowrie (Boston, 1956); and Eduard Giesmar, *Lectures on the Religious Thought of Søren Kierkegaard* (Minneapolis, 1937), 63–97.

[11] Sverdrup, *Samlede skrifter*, 3:360.

[12] Here and two paragraphs below, see Nelson and Fevold, *Lutheran Church Among Norwegian-Americans*, 1:17–21, 40, 164–168; 2:18, 146.

[13] Here and below, see Sverdrup, *Samlede skrifter*, 2:288–311.

[14] Here and two paragraphs below, see Sverdrup, *Samlede skrifter*, 2:295, 298–303.

[15] Here and below, see Sverdrup, *Samlede skrifter*, 2:303–311, 316.

[16] Bodensieck, *Encyclopedia of the Lutheran Church*, 1:659–664.

[17] Here and below, see Bodensieck, *Encyclopedia of the Lutheran Church*, 1:659–664; Sverdrup, *Samlede skrifter*, 4:1–50; Fevold, *The Lutheran Free Church*, 130.

[18] Sverdrup, *Samlede skrifter*, 4:12, 28.

[19] Here and two paragraphs below, see N. N. Rønning and W. H. Lien, *They Followed Him: The Lutheran Deaconess Home and Hospital, Fiftieth Anniversary, 1889–1939* (Minneapolis, 1939), 37–42. See also Sverdrup, *Samlede skrifter*, 4:1–50, and Fevold, *The Lutheran Free Church*, 130. The name of the corporation was changed to the Lutheran Deaconess Home and Hospital in 1923.

[20] Here and below, see *Beretning af forenede Kirke*, 1890, 145–150; Sverdrup, *Samlede skrifter*, 4:1–50; Rønning and Lien, *They Followed Him*, 48–57; Fevold, *The Lutheran Free Church*, 131; Emil Wacker, *Diakonissegjerningen i fortid og nutid*, trans. Georg Sverdrup (Minneapolis, 1898).

[21] Here and below, see Sverdrup, *Samlede skrifter*, 4:23, 26, 37–46; Rønning and Lien, *They Followed Him*, 43.

[22] Mead, *Lively Experiment*, 175–183. Carnegie's famous essay, published in 1889, expressed some of the ideas scholars have associated with the term "social Darwinism," including the application of "survival of the fittest" to the economic sphere.

[23] Kenneth Scott Latourette, *A History of Christianity* (New York, 1953), 1032–1033.

[24] Here and below, see James Hastings Nichols, *History of Christianity, 1650–1950: Secularization of the West* (New York, 1956), 306–320; Bodensieck, *Encyclopedia of the Lutheran Church*, 1:9–24, 537–538; Sverdrup, *Samlede skrifter*, 1:222.

[25] Here and below, see Sverdrup, *Samlede skrifter*, 1:225–227, and 6:ix.

[26] See selections from these reports included in Sverdrup, *Samlede skrifter*, 3:311–346. The reports cover the years 1899–1906.

[27] Sverdrup, *Samlede skrifter*, 6. See also Sverdrup, *Samlede skrifter*, 3:329, and Fevold, *The Lutheran Free Church*, 121–124.

[28] Sverdrup, *Samlede skrifter*, 4:54–56.

[29] Sverdrup, *Samlede skrifter*, 4:51–53. The lecture, entitled "Missionens betydning for menigheden," is included in Sverdrup, *Samlede skrifter*, 2:362–370.

[30] Sverdrup, *Samlede skrifter*, 2:368.

[31] Nelson, *The Lutherans in North America*, 128–159, 210–238, 305–313.

[32] Sverdrup, *Samlede skrifter*, 3:340.

Chapter Nine

[1] G. F. Heiberg, *Slekten Heiberg* (Oslo, 1941), 286–296; Sverdrup, *Samlede skrifter*, 3:91; Helland, *Georg Sverdrup*, 232; *Beretning af Konferentsen*, 1888, 11. Cathrine E. Heiberg was born November 4, 1853.

[2] Elise Welhaven Gunnersen, "Memoirs," 136–144, manuscript in Norwegian-American Historical Association Archives, Northfield.

[3] Gunnersen, "Memoirs," 144–235.

[4] Heiberg, *Slekten Heiberg*, 286–296; Helland, *Georg Sverdrup*, 232.

⁵ *Beretning af Konferentsen*, 1888, 11; Helland, *Georg Sverdrup*, 233.

⁶ John H. Blegen, "Biografiske optegnelser for mine barn," 212, hereafter cited as "Memoirs." Manuscript is in Minnesota Historical Society Archives, St. Paul, photocopy in Augsburg College Archives.

⁷ Heiberg, *Slekten Heiberg*, 286–296; Helland, *Georg Sverdrup*, 233. Elisa Susanne Heiberg was born October 17, 1864. Additional information on the Sverdrup family was provided by George M. Sverdrup, July, 1985, notes in author's possession.

⁸ These letters, the sources for this and the next six paragraphs, have been preserved in the Augsburg College Archives.

⁹ Information on the Sverdrup family provided by George M. Sverdrup, July, 1985. The following names are included in that information: *Son*: George Sverdrup; *Grandsons*: George Sverdrup Michaelsen, George Marshall Sverdrup, George Sverdrup Bergh; *Great-Grandsons*: George Sverdrup Michaelsen, George Edward Ellison, George Michael Sverdrup, George Sverdrup Bergh; *Great-Great Grandsons*: Per Georg Sverdrup, David George Bergh, George Sverdrup Bergh.

¹⁰ Helland, *Georg Sverdrup*, 111; Gunnersen, "Memoirs," 136–235, 260.

¹¹ Rønning, *Fifty Years in America*, 141, 145; Nelson and Fevold, *Lutheran Church Among Norwegian-Americans*, 1:223; Theodore C. Blegen, *The Saga of Saga Hill* (St. Paul, 1971), 17; Helland, *Georg Sverdrup*, 244; John H. Blegen, "Memoirs," 211. This statement concerning Sverdrup is quoted in Theodore C. Blegen, *The Saga of Saga Hill*, 22.

¹² Gunnersen, "Memoirs," 208, 225; Helland, *Georg Sverdrup*, 234; Sverdrup, *Samlede skrifter*, 3:45, 81.

¹³ Blegen, *The Saga of Saga Hill*, 11–21.

¹⁴ The letter has been preserved in Augsburg College Archives with an English translation by Agnes B. Tangjerd. See also Helland, *Georg Sverdrup*, 241.

¹⁵ The letters cited may be found in the Augsburg College Archives. The letter from Sverdrup to Pastor Berlie is dated February 9, 1906.

¹⁶ Helland, *Georg Sverdrup*, 275–281; *Folkebladet*, May 8, 1907. See also Chrislock, *From Fjord to Freeway*, 90. N. N. Rønning referred to Oftedal's farewell words as he placed a wreath on Sverdrup's coffin as "one of the most dramatic incidents I ever witnessed;" Rønning, *Fifty Years in America*, 147.

Chapter Ten

¹ John O. Evjen, "What is Lutheranism?" in Vergilius Ferm, ed., *What Is Lutheranism? A Symposium in Interpretation* (New York, 1930), 9.

² Vergilius Ferm spoke of Evjen as "one of Lutheran America's most able theologians"; see Ferm, *What Is Lutheranism?*, 7. Evjen published articles on Sverdrup in English, German, and Norwegian. For a brief assessment of Evjen's contributions, see James S. Hamre, "John O. Evjen: Teacher, Theologian, Biographer," in *Concordia Historical Institute Quarterly*, 47:2 (Summer, 1974), 52–61. A thorough discussion of Evjen's life and thought is given in Arthur J. Tolo, "The Doctrine of the Church in the

Teaching of John Oluf Evjen" (Ph.D. dissertation, Chicago Lutheran Theological Seminary, 1951).

[3] Here and below, see Schlesinger, "A Critical Period in American Protestantism," 523–548. See also Mead, *The Lively Experiment*, 134–187.

[4] Two examples of persons who came from Norway and made tours of Norwegian settlements in America, in which they propounded some of these advanced views, were Bjørnstjerne Bjørnson and Kristofer Janson. See Eva Lund Haugen and Einar Haugen, trans. and eds., *Land of the Free: Bjørnstjerne Bjørnson's America Letters, 1880–1881* (Northfield, Minnesota, 1978), 139–245; and Draxten, *Kristofer Janson in America*, 3–41.

[5] Michaelsen, "The Protestant Ministry in America," 269.

[6] Rønning, *Fifty Years in America*, 146.

[7] The undated newspaper clipping, which appears to be from the *Minneapolis Tribune*, is in the Augsburg College Archives.

[8] Speaking of developments in theological education in America since 1850, Robert Michaelsen states that there was a tendency for such education to become "increasingly pragmatic." He goes on to say that the education of ministers, "like education in general, has moved away from the classical pattern toward a greater emphasis on practical arts and vocational training. An obvious evidence of this shift is seen in the gradual de-emphasis of classical language study." Michaelsen, "The Protestant Ministry in America," 274.

[9] Sverdrup, *Samlede skrifter*, 3:88; Chrislock, *From Fjord to Freeway*, 117, 137.

[10] See Warren Quanbeck's "Introduction," in Helland, *Heritage of Faith*, 4–6. See also Nelson and Fevold, *Lutheran Church Among Norwegian-Americans*, 2:285.

[11] Ousland, *En kirkehøvding*, 43.

[12] Evjen, "Georg Sverdrup," in Hauck, *Real-Encyclopädie*, 24:541

[13] Ousland, *En kirkehøvding*, 300–309; Aarflot, *Norsk kirkehistorie*, 2:417; Molland, "Endringer i det religiøse liv," 1:502.

[14] Perry Miller, *Errand into the Wilderness* (Cambridge, Massachussetts, 1956), especially chapter one.

[15] See "Vort Folk og vor Kirke," in *Lutheraneren og Missionsbladet*, 15:2 (January, 1881), 27–29. No author is listed for the article, but it was published during the time Sverdrup served as editor of the journal and its style and content have led the author to ascribe it to him. James S. Hamre, "Georg Sverdrup's 'Errand into the Wilderness': Building the 'Free and Living' Congregation," in *Concordia Historical Institute Quarterly*, 53:1 (Spring, 1980), 39–47, discusses in greater detail the philosophy of history that motivated Sverdrup.

[16] Sverdrup, *Samlede skrifter*, 3:7, 15, 24–28.

[17] Scholars have pointed out that the theme of a "new beginning" was a prominent one among Protestants in America during the nineteenth century. See Mead, *The Lively Experiment*, 110. The Semmingsen reference is to her *Veien mot vest*, 2:50.

[18] *Norsk biografisk leksikon*, 15:409. Koht's statement reads "han var alltid viss paa at han var i pakt med fremtiden."

Index